PASSAGES:
A Guide for Pilgrims of the Mind

PASSAGES:
A Guide for Pilgrims of the Mind

by
Marianne S. Andersen
and
Louis M. Savary

Consulting Editors

STANLEY KRIPPNER, Ph.D.
Director, Dream Laboratory,
Maimonides Medical Center

MILTON V. KLINE, Ph.D.
Director, Institute for Research in Hypnosis
and of the Morton Prince Clinic
for Hypnotherapy

A Collins Associates Book

HARPER & ROW, PUBLISHERS

New York, Hagerstown, San Francisco, London

STANDARD BOOK NUMBER: 06-067065-7

LIBRARY OF CONGRESS CATALOG CARD
NUMBER: 72-78056

Acknowledgments

Many of the works from which selections herein are taken are protected by copyright, and may not be reproduced in any form without the consent of the authors, their publishers, or their agents. Every effort has been made to trace the ownership of all selections in this book and to obtain the necessary authorization for their use. If any errors or omissions have occurred in this regard, corrections will be made in all future editions of this book. Since the copyright page cannot legibly accommodate all the acknowledgments and copyright notices, this page and the pages following constitute an extension of the copyright page.

Allan Angoff, selections from *The Psychic Force*, G. P. Putnam's Sons, copyright©1970 by Parapsychology Foundation.

W. H. Auden, selection from *The Age of Anxiety*, Random House, copyright©1947 by W. H. Auden.

Joan Baez, selection from *Dream*, copyright©1969 by Dial Press.

Sir William Barrett, quoted in *The Psychic Force*, ed. by Allan Angoff, G. P. Putnam's Sons, copyright©1970 Parapsychology Foundation.

Basho, selections from *Zeami, Basho, Yeats, Pound* by Makoto Ueda, Mouton & Co., Publishers, The Hague; from *Japanese Literature* by Donald Keene, Grove Press, Inc., copyright©1955 by Donald Keene; and from *The Narrow Road to the Deep North and Other Travel Sketches*, Penguin Books Ltd.

Bernard Berenson, selection from *Sketch for a Self-Portrait*, copyright©1949 by Pantheon Books.

Henri Bergson, selection from *Dreams*, translated by Edwin E. Slosson, copyright©1914 by B. W. Huebsch.

Leonard Bernstein, selections from *The Infinite Variety of Music*, Simon and Schuster, Inc., copyright© 1966 Leonard Bernstein Foundation, Inc.

Paul Bindrim, selections from "Facilitating Peak Experiences" in *Ways of Growth: Approaches to Expanding Awareness*, ed. by Herbert Otto and John Mann, Grossman Publishers, copyright©1968 by Herbert Otto and John Mann. Reprinted by permission of Grossman Publishers.

Black Elk, selection from *The Sacred Pipe* by Joseph Epes Brown, copyright©1953 by University of Oklahoma Press.

Leon Bloy, selection from *Pilgrim of the Absolute*, ed. by Raissa Maritain, copyright©1947 by Pantheon Books.

Dietrich Bonhoeffer, selection from *Letters and Papers from Prison*, copyright©1954 by The Macmillan Company.

Helen L. Bonny, selections taken from "The Use of Music in Psychedelic (LSD) Psychotherapy" by Helen L. Bonny and Walter N. Pahnke, *Journal of Music Therapy*, June 1972, copyright©1972 by The National Association for Music Therapy.

Murray Bookchin, selection from *Post-Scarcity Anarchism*, Ramparts Books, copyright©1971 by Murray Bookchin.

William Braden, selection from *The Private Sea LSD and the Search for God*, Quadrangle Books, Inc., copyright©1967 by William Braden.

Norman O. Brown, selections from "A Reply to Herbert Marcuse" in *Commentary*, March 1967, copyright©1967 by American Jewish Committee; and from *Life Against Death*, copyright©1959 Wesleyan University.

Richard M. Bucke, selections from *Cosmic Consciousness*, copyright©1923 by E. P. Dutton & Co., Inc.

Arthur Butler, quoted in *Einstein—The Life and Times* by Ronald W. Clark, World Publishing Company, copyright©1971 by Ronald W. Clark.

Robert N. Butler, selection from "Age: The Life Review" in *Psychology Today*, December, 1971, copyright© 1971 by Communications Research Machines, Inc.

James Carroll, selections from "Contemplation" in the *National Catholic Reporter*, December 3, 1971; from "The Right to Ritual" in the *National Catholic Reporter*, Dec. 17, 1971; and from "The Counter Culture Contemplates" in the *National Catholic Reporter*, December 24, 1971.

Lewis Carroll, selections from *Through the Looking Glass*, in *The Works of Lewis Carroll*, Hamlyn Publishing Group Ltd., copyright©1965 by Hamlyn Publishing Group Ltd.

Henri Charrière, selection from *Papillon*, copyright©1970 by William Morrow & Co., Inc.

Jean Cocteau, selection from "The Process of Inspiration" from *Le Foyer des Artistes*.

Eleanor Criswell, selections from "What Meditation Can Do For You" in *New Woman*, November, 1971, copyright©1971 by Allied Publications, Inc.

Eric Cuddon, selections from "The Relief of Pain by Laying on of Hands: Suggestion? Restoration of Electrostatic Balance? Emanation? Illusion?" in the *International Journal of Parapsychology*, Vol. X, No. 1, Spring, 1968.

(Acknowledgments continued on page 222)

CONTENTS

RELATING

TRANSCENDING

Foreword

The history of the United States is a history of a people concerned with external voyages. At first, the exploration and settlement of the continent occupied their attention. This was followed by the development of industrial empires at home and the assertion of diplomatic power overseas. Currently, the adventure of outer space continues to direct America's energy in external directions.

In recent years, however, a growing number of Americans have placed a high priority on internal events and inner growth. Some individuals view this as a spiritual quest; others consider it a voyage of self-discovery or a search for personal identity. Most of them speak of "human potential," "peak experiences," and "altered states of consciousness." These people have a driving need to explore the far reaches of the psyche in order to participate more fully in life's adventure.

The roads taken in attainment of this goal vary. Some seek the short-cuts offered by psychedelic chemicals; others study Yoga, Zen, transcendental meditation, or some other spiritual discipline.

Many people favor group settings at growth centers (such as Esalen) or with like-minded members of organizations (such as the Association for Research and Enlightenment). Others take solitary paths, keeping diaries of their dreams and their most intensive experiences, or embarking on personal reading and study programs.

For one type of individual, the road to enlightenment may be austere, as he fasts, prays, and communes with nature in the forests or deserts. For another type, the road is one of passion and ecstasy involving sensual experience and sexual encounters.

In every instance, the going will be smoother if the voyager has a guide to point out what other travelers have found in the past. This function may be served by a Zen master, a psychotherapist, a religious teacher, an esteemed friend, or a guidebook such as holy scripture, *The Tibetan Book of the Dead,* the *I Ching,* or the writings of Sri Aurobindo, A.H. Maslow, Alan Watts, St. Teresa, or Kahil Gibran.

In its own modest way, it is hoped that *Passages* will be such a guide. It need not be the only source of help to an individual on an inner search, but it may well play a decisive role in a person's growth and development. *Passages* came into being as larger and larger numbers of Americans set off on the journey for authenticity, personal integration, and self-awareness.

Thus, *Passages* may be thought of as a road map. It may not serve for everyone's trip, but its creation will be justified if it prevents even one hard-pressed pilgrim from taking a wrong path, or from falling along the way.

Stanley Krippner

Introduction

A Map of the Mind

The mind is a vast, uncharted territory and most of us never penetrate into its rich hinterland. We are not aware that what we call normal consciousness is living only on the fringe of an immense land. *Passages* invites you to become a pilgrim of the mind and explore all its dimensions, as you enter into ASC (altered states of consciousness).

The key to the entire process is to find the passages or pathways to ASC. Once Columbus had discovered how to get to America, the passage was found and others followed the trail he blazed across the ocean. Over the centuries there have been many Columbuses searching for and finding new worlds of the mind. From what they have discovered and experienced it is now possible to make a map of the mind. Naturally, this map does not have clarity and detail, but it does point the way to uncharted lands.

Pilgrims of the mind can be reassured that others have gone before them, they are not journeying into the totally unknown. However, the altered state of each particular individual's own consciousness is for him a new, unmapped world. The exploration of that world is his own experience, similar to the experiences of others but

Potential Forms of Consciousness

Our normal waking consciousness, rational consciousness as we call it, is but one special type of consciousness, whilst all about it, parted from it by the filmiest of screens, there lie potential forms of consciousness entirely different . . . No account of the universe in its totality can be final which leaves these other forms of consciousness quite disregarded. . . . they forbid a premature closing of our accounts with reality.

William James

Any Land You Choose

Bid your soul travel to any land you choose and sooner than you bid it go, it will be there. Bid it fly up to heaven, and it will not lack for wings. Nothing can bar its way, neither the fiery heat of the sun, nor the swirl of the planet-spheres. Cleaving its way through all, it will fly up till it reaches the outermost of all corporeal things. And should you wish to break forth from the universe itself and gaze on the things outside the cosmos, even that is permitted to you. See what power, what quickness is yours.

Hermes Trismegistus

Reports from a New Country

For, just as medieval explorers brought home the news that there existed lands which their fellow-countrymen had never seen, and probably never would see, but the existence of which they would henceforward take on trust, so the mystics, one after another, with a unanimity independent of age, creed or race, bring us reports from a country, more difficult to chart than any on earth, which, but for their testimony, might be supposed to exist only in the imagination.

E. Allison Peers

The Mind's Window

Our discipline is the unknown; the mind has a window toward infinity.

Sidney Parnes

A World of Inner Space

When one turns his attention inward, he discovers a world of "inner space" which is as vast and as "real" as the external, physical world. Through exploring this inner world, each of us potentially has access to vast realms of knowledge through his own mind, including secrets of the universe so far known only to a very few. And the deepest desire of man is to know himself and to experience his relationship to the universe about him.

Subject's evaluation
from Willis W. Harman
The Psychedelic Experience

The Explorer's Achievement

It is true that the traveler, equipped with a detailed map of a region across which he plans his itinerary, enjoys a striking intellectual superiority over the explorer who first enters a new region—yet the explorer's fumbling progress is a much finer achievement than the well-briefed traveler's journey. Even if we admitted that an exact knowledge of the universe is our supreme mental possession it would still follow that man's most distinguished act of thought consists in producing such knowledge; the human mind is at its greatest when it brings hitherto unchartered domains under its control. Such operations renew the existing articulate framework. Hence they cannot be performed within this framework but have to rely (to this extent) on the kind of plunging reorientation which we share with the animals. Fundamental novelty can be discovered only by the same tacit powers which rats use in learning a maze.

Michael Polanyi

unique for him. Like the first pioneers who set out across the continent of America, he will discover a whole, new, exciting land.

Many, today, feel drawn towards the exploration of higher states of consciousness. A most obvious manifestation of this desire can be seen in the use of LSD and other drugs to produce a "high" which is an altered state of consciousness. Drug experiences have alerted people to the fact that there are other dimensions of the mind beyond what we call rational consciousness. Can they be attained without the use of drugs? Emphatically— Yes! *Passages* offers the opportunity to begin to explore your unknown mind, without drugs.

True Awakening

The aim of the game is true awakening, full development of the powers latent in man. The game can be played only by people whose observations of themselves and others have led them to a certain conclusion, namely, that man's ordinary state of consciousness, his so-called waking state, is not the highest level of consciousness of which he is capable. In fact, this state is so far from real awakening that it could appropriately be called a form of somnambulism, a condition of "waking sleep."

Robert S. DeRopp

A Transformation in Depth

Since the development of life means the rise and growth of consciousness, that development could not continue indefinitely along its own line without a transformation in depth: like all great developments in the world, life had to become different in order to remain itself.

Pierre Teilhard de Chardin

The More Alive Person

The more a person is able to direct his life consciously, the more he can use time for constructive benefits. The more, however, that he is conformist, unfree, undifferentiated, the more, that is, he works not by choice but by compulsion, the more he is then the object of quantitative time ... The less alive a person is—"alive" here defined as having conscious direction of his life—the more is time for him the time of the clock. The more alive he is, the more he lives by qualitative time.

Rollo May

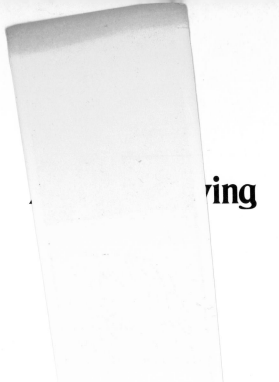

...ving

Passag... ...or parlor games, or weird ... ...e mind exercises intended ... ...ore fully aware way of life. ... ...between being able to play ... ...a professional concert pia... ...any people merely play at living without ever becoming fully alive. The suggestions for thinking and behaving in this book can become a new way of life, or, from another viewpoint, a way of spirituality.

When techniques of hypnosis, hypnotherapy, and dream research treat the altered state of consciousness as a specialized, extraordinary and momentary state of being, the inference is that what we have called ordinary consciousness is the normal way people should live. *Passages* challenges this inference and suggests that ordinary consciousness is a limited experience, a two-dimensional flatland, while the altered state of consciousness, a three-dimensional space is, in fact, the consciousness intended for mankind.

To speak of *Passages* as a way of living is not far-fetched. It has, in fact, been suggested and predicted by some of today's outstanding thinkers. Teilhard de Chardin's evolutionary theory envisages man reaching out toward new levels of

A Re-visiting of History

And so it all comes down to the same thing in the end, whether we start with the technological fantasies of Herman Kahn, the mysticism of Edgar Cayce, or the cosmic fictions of Arthur C. Clarke. Western Civilization is drawing to a close in an age of apocalyptic turmoil in which the old species, collectivizing mankind with machines, and the new species, unifying it in consciousness, are in collusion with one another to end what we know as human nature. Western man will no doubt try to prove that he is not merely mud to be shaped into bricks for the dreamers' temples, but even taking the conservative obstinacy of industrial man into account, it would still seem that we are at one of those moments when the whole meaning of nature, self, and civilization is overturned in a re-visioning of history as important as any technological innovation.

William Irwin Thompson

The Fastest Way

It might turn out that exploring the far-out spaces of human consciousness is the fastest way to social transformation.

John C. Lilly

Untapped Potential

Each person has a wide range of innate potentialities that remain untapped. Whether physical or mental, these potentialities can become expressed only to the extent that circumstances are favorable to their existential manifestation . . . One can take it for granted that the latent potentialities of human beings have a better chance to become actualized when the social environment is sufficiently diversified to provide a variety of stimulating experiences.

René Jules Dubos

Living in the Light

Enough that the new awareness is abroad, emerging simultaneously in many places like flowers in the spring, beneath the ugly wreckage of a past civilization. For the discontent of youth is, in my view, an expression of a widespread and growing determination to reconstruct our way of living in the light of a new and richer conception of what man is and should be.

Lancelot Law Whyte

Dimensions of the Universe

To the common sense of the "man in the street" and even to a certain philosophy of the world to which nothing is possible save what has always been, perspectives such as these will seem highly improbable. But to a mind become familiar with the fantastic dimensions of the universe they will, on the contrary, seem quite natural, because they are directly proportionate with astronomical immensities.

Pierre Teilhard de Chardin

New Categories of Thinking

All these phenomena must be viewed, however, as aspects of the underlying and unconscious movement in modern times toward the development of a new ideology. This means more than a new system of beliefs; it means basic new categories of cognition by which the outer and inner experiences of modern life can be perceived and interpreted. The popular movements of the past decade that are sociologically related to the growth of interest in parapsychology are very significant steps toward the development of a new world view.

Ira Progoff

complexity-consciousness. One of the characteristics of man at this level will be the ability of a group of people to think-together, love-together.

John C. Lilly speaks of mind exploration and levels of experiencing, so that life is lived in a more intense or "turned-on" way. Lilly also suggests that there is no reason why people should not live continually at a level of consciousness that they may have experienced only momentarily. He is of the opinion that the chief reason that people fail to do this is their ignorance of the way into that state of consciousness.

Passages was written to help people discover the pathways, or doors, that lead into these altered states of consciousness. The exercises suggest ways in which the exploration of altered states of consciousness can enrich the lives of individuals. Some of the exercises have a purely practical purpose, others are highly transcendental. *Passages* also assumes that the insights gained from altered states of consciousness will give a new and more creative direction to life. The book opens the way to a potential source of new energy. That energy can be harnessed to all that is positive and creative in human living, but it can also be dissipated and wasted in the explosion of violence. *Passages* invites its readers to harness that energy and realize in themselves a potential that has too long been dormant.

The Little Golden Key

Alice was not a bit hurt, and she jumped up on her feet in a moment: she looked up, but it was all dark overhead: before her was another long passage, and the White Rabbit was still in sight, hurrying down it. There was not a moment to be lost: away went Alice like the wind, and was just in time to hear it say, as it turned a corner, 'Oh my ears and whiskers, how late it's getting!' She was close behind it when she turned the corner, but the Rabbit was no longer to be seen: she found herself in a long, low hall, which was lit up by a row of lamps hanging from the roof.

There were doors all round the hall, but they were all locked: and when Alice had been all the way down one side and up the other, trying every door, she walked sadly down the middle, wondering how she was ever to get out again.

Suddenly she came upon a little three-legged table, all made of solid glass: there was nothing on it but a tiny golden key, and Alice's first idea was that this might belong to one of the doors of the hall; but, alas! either the locks were too large, or the key was too small, but at any rate it would not open any of them. However, on the second time round, she came upon a low curtain she had not noticed before, and behind it was a little door about fifteen inches high: she tried the little golden key in the lock, and to her great delight it fitted!

Lewis Carroll
Through the Looking Glass

Trance Induction

The first problem in all psychological experience involving unexplored dimensions of the mind is how to discover the *passage* or pathway into them. Many different techniques can be used to induce altered states of consciousness. The most highly publicized technique is drugs but there are many others being developed. Bio-feedback studies show that *electronic patterning* can be used to induce creative states of consciousness. Recent psychological experimentation has used *perceptual alteration* which includes forms of sensory deprivation, sensory overload and equilibrium distortion. Another category of *suggestion-teaching* involves hypnotists, guides or gurus who induce trance states in their subjects during face-to-face encounters or by means of recordings. Finally, there are *self-induction* techniques that involve only the subject and use no equipment.

Passages presents self-induction techniques in order to make it possible for anyone willing to learn the necessary skills to enter into altered states of consciousness. No drugs are involved, there is no need for expensive equipment or for a hypnotist or guru. All that is required is the patience and discipline to practice the exercises. The exercises may differ but the first two steps in all of them are the same. They are *relaxation* and *concentration*.

For Any Creative Person

The guy who invents a way of inducing a creative trance is going to make a fortune because this is something that any creative person would give his right arm for.

Leonard Bernstein

Allow Yourself

There are
worlds
beyond universes
to which you
rarely allow yourself
to travel.

Know there
go there
there there.

Bernard Gunther

What a Man Thinks

The transmigration of life takes place in one's mind. Let one therefore keep the mind pure, for what a man thinks, that he becomes.

Upanishads

The Subconscious

The subconscious mind plays a very important part in the interior life, even though it remains behind the scenes. Just as a good play depends on the scene, the lighting, and all the rest, so too our interior life owes much of its character to the setting and lighting and background and atmosphere which are provided, without any deliberate action of our own, by our subconscious mind.

Thomas Merton

23

Relaxation

Undivided Concentration

To concentrate in this undivided way you first give yourself a "suggestion" to the effect that you will relax your mind and your body, making the body insensitive and the mind a blank, and yet reserving the power to "break" the concentration in a short time. By making the body insensitive I mean simply to relax completely your mental hold of, or awareness of, all bodily sensation. After giving yourself this suggestion a few times, you proceed to relax both body and mind. Relax all mental interest in everything in the environment; inhibit all thoughts which try to wander into consciousness from the subconsciousness, or from wherever else thoughts come. This is clearly a more thorough affair than "just relaxing."

Mrs. Upton Sinclair

Getting Rid of Strain

There may be strain to start with, but it is getting rid of strain, both physical and mental, which constitutes relaxation, or blankness, of the conscious mind. Practice will teach you what this state is, and after a while you can achieve it without strain.

Mrs. Upton Sinclair

The term relaxation is used here in a very different sense from its usual colloquial meaning. It does not mean a flaccid state of muscles or letting yourself flop. Rather, it is a state of complete muscular equilibrium and poise.

In *This Magic Body,* Jennette Lee suggests that the human body should naturally be experienced as if in a state of weightlessness. Not that bodies should float in the air or that weighing machines should not register when people stand on them. Rather, what Lee is talking about is muscular balance. Muscles come in pairs—one muscle pulls to the right, its partner pulls to the left; one pulls up, its partner pulls down. When muscles are in perfect equilibrium and co-ordination the body has a sense of weightlessness. It is ready to do gracefully, effortlessly, whatever the mind asks it to do. Mind and body are in perfect accord and harmony. They are working *together.*

Lee maintains that this state of accord between mind and body, perfectly attuned and balanced in themselves and toward each other, should be the natural state of human living. Tiredness, strain, gritting one's teeth, making efforts of will, far from being normal is in reality an emergency situation for mind-body. But only when we realize the possibility of a higher state of consciousness can we recognize the emergency for what it is. Preparatory to entering into altered states of consciousness it is essential to learn how to relax so that mind and body are in harmony and free from imbalance and tensions. Many people have experienced this harmony quite naturally, but only for brief periods. However, with practice it is possible to be habitually relaxed, in muscular equilibrium, as a permanent state. A ballet dancer has to achieve this. A skilled pianist has no need consciously to will his fingers to move. The music flows out of him without effort. The exercises and training that pregnant women undergo in preparation for natural childbirth constitute a discipline resulting in muscular equilibrium and harmony between mind and body. It is also a known fact that jogging for many miles, far from being tiring, can actually produce a sense of weightlessness, a feeling of being able to go on forever.

Learning to relax may at first be a consciously controlled process but after practice and training the controls become so much a part of a person that he is not aware of them. He will then relax naturally and easily with mind-body perfectly coordinated and responsive to each other.

The Starting Point

Standing **also offers rich possibilities for sensing experiments. Alone the restoration to fuller functioning of the bare foot (which in flexibility and sentitivity is far nearer to the hand than we usually realize) offers great rewards. Standing is the starting point of greatest potential for physical activity, from which walking, running, fighting, dancing and all sports begin and to which they return. It is the specifically human activity, which is exploited by all the less civilized peoples and by children who have not yet abandoned its uses and pleasures for the chimera of "relaxation." Easy and balanced standing, in which our inner reactiveness mobilizes precisely the energy needed to counterbalance the pull of the earth, permits a full sensing of the total organism.**

Charlotte Selver

Move into any Space

Once you know a space exists you can learn to get back to it. You can program yourself to move into any space you know exists if you use discipline and concentration.

John C. Lilly

Focusing the Mind

Meditation is a mental practice which can have any number of physical activities correlated with it, but is essentially a question of focusing the mind. You begin by focusing your mind, or concentrating, which takes practice. As you are successfully able to concentrate and clear your mind, you gradually enter a state of consciousness which some have called the fourth state of consciousness, meditation.

This state of consciousness has been characterized by relaxed awareness and receptivity. If you remain in the meditative state long enough you enter a state of union or identification with what you are meditating on. This state is called samadhi in yoga.

Eleanor Criswell

Concentration

A Different Kind of Concentration

The first thing you have to do is to learn the trick of undivided attention or concentration. By these terms I mean something quite different from what is ordinarily meant. One "concentrates" on writing a chapter in a book, or on solving a problem in mathematics; but this is a complicated process of dividing one's attention, giving it to one detail after another, judging, balancing, making decisions. The kind of concentration I mean is putting the attention on one object, or one uncomplicated thought, such as joy, or peace, and holding it there steadily. It isn't thinking; it is inhibiting thought, except for one thought, or one object of thought. You have to inhibit the impulse to think things about the object, to examine it, or appraise it, or to allow memory-trains to attach themselves to it. The average person has never heard of such a form of concentration, and so has to learn how to do it. Simultaneously, he must learn to relax, for strangely enough, a part of concentration is complete relaxation.

Mrs. Upton Sinclair

Concentration also has a very special meaning in the context of inducing altered states of consciousness. It does not connote the usual intellectual tautness that people associate with concentration. On the contrary it involves little intellectual activity and is more a process of focusing the mind on an object as simply and as quietly as you would focus a camera lens.

Or, to put it another way, the type of concentration required is that of a small child who becomes absorbed in what he is looking at—a flower, an insect, a bird. His attention to it is not simply an intellectual exercise but rather a centering of all his faculties on the object.

Only the Eye

Once in ancient India there was a tournament held to test marksmanship in archery. A wooden fish was set up on a high pole and the eye of the fish was the target. One by one many valiant princes came and tried their skill, but in vain. Before each one shot his arrow the teacher asked him what he saw, and invariably all replied that they saw a fish on a pole at a great height with head, eyes, etc.; but Arjuna, as he took his aim, said: "I see the eye of the fish," and he was the only one who succeeded in hitting the mark.

Paramananda

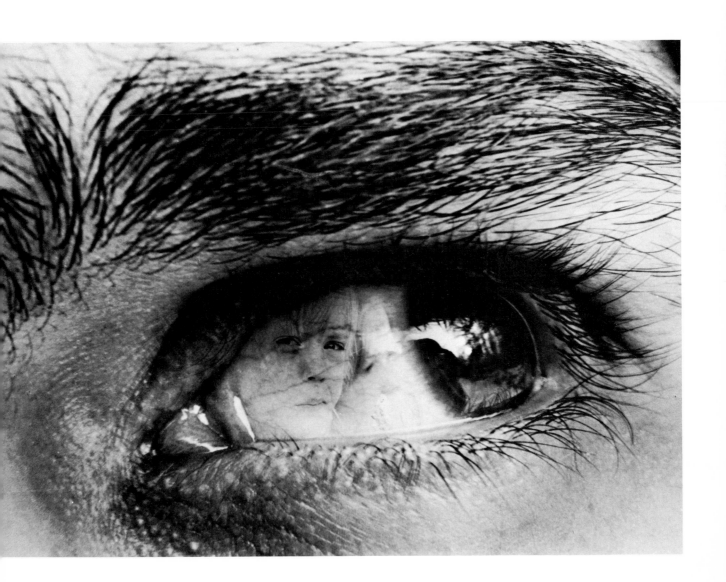

A Continuum of Control

Willed Decontrol

This one point, that spontaneity depends on good controls, including the control manifested in the ability voluntarily to abandon control, casts particular light on creativeness in mystical experience. Here the single aim of control is decontrol, and the willed decontrol is all.

Stephen M. Schoen

For the Uncontrolled

For the uncontrolled there is no wisdom, nor for the uncontrolled is there the power of concentration; and for him without concentration there is no peace. And for the unpeaceful, how can there be happiness?

The Bhagavadgita

Those who engage in *Passages* exercises are normally at some point along a continuum of control. At one end of the continuum is the *controlled* person, the classic Apollonian personality: very rational, not subject to impulse, who, at all times, knows what he is doing and considers it essential to decide and choose, in almost all circumstances, what he will do and how he will behave.

At the other end of the continuum is the person who may be described as *suggestible,* the classic Dionysian personality: spontaneous, impulsive, happy-go-lucky, who does not give high priority to controlling behavior and actions.

Welcoming the Body Back

We are proposing welcoming the body back into the union with the self. This means as already suggested recovering an active awareness of one's body. It means experiencing one's body—the pleasure of eating or resting or the exhilaration of using toned-up muscles or the gratification of sexual impulses and passion—as aspects of the acting self. It is not the attitude of "My body feels" but "I feel."

Rollo May

Within and Without

Only when energetic control of the mind-body, within and without, gives way to synergetic control and functioning, does the mind-body become a normal effective instrument for generating power to shape new forms of life. Only when we begin to see what the mind-body is really like and are ready to let it function as it is constructed to function, can we reasonably expect it to develop its latent power to create new forms or new uses of its present form.

Jennette Lee

Learning to Let Go

If I cannot say it clearly and simply, it is because I am not master of my instrument, because I have not learned in my whole mind-body—in my muscles, brain, and nerves—how to focus-and-let-go in the same breath. I have not learned how to focus my mind to the truth that has come to me through experience, and at the same instant trust to a vital experience of letting-go, to give it shape.

Jennette Lee

The "Other Me"

Whenever self-consciousness is subdued, when the known and claimant "me" retires to the background, then an opportunity is afforded for the emergence of the "other me" of that large and unrecognized part of our personality which lies below the threshold of our consciousness.

Sir William Barrett

Habits of Tension

Life might be altogether different for middle-aged people, were we taught autonomic control in kindergarten, for the habits of tension that may evolve into disease might be caught early and prevented.

Gay Luce and Erik Peper

Suggestion

Suggestion does not consist in making an individual believe what is not true: suggestion consists in making something come true by making him believe in its possibility.

J. A. Hadfield

Men who can dream

We need men who can dream of things that never were, and ask why not.

George Bernard Shaw

Passages will be attractive to both personality types. The controlled person can be reassured that he will be still in control of himself in altered states of consciousness, that he will have some sort of map of the mind. He will also have some advance notice about the kinds of experiences to expect. Finally, he will have the assurance that he will be able to return from an altered state of consciousness, just as he will enter, when he chooses.

The controlled person may at first be reluctant to make the initial passage into an altered state of consciousness. He will probably have to work hard and long for his first success; but once he has reached an altered state of consciousness he will probably be the best subject for the self-induced approach of *Passages*.

The suggestible person, on the other hand, may find the passage into an altered state of consciousness almost immediately. However, he may become frightened when he finds himself alone in an unknown dimension. The suggestible person may have much more success with *Passages* if he has a guide, at the beginning, to whom he can entrust himself with confidence.

One who is psychologically unbalanced or insecure may run the risk of harming his psyche and perhaps initiating a process of ego fragmentation if he performs the exercises without a guide. Such a one should perform *Passages* exercises only under the direction of a professional psychotherapist, preferably one with expert knowledge of hypnosis.

Allowing Us to Hear

We turn on a radio and hear
an orchestra playing
Vienna Bonbons,
and of course the music was there
in the room all the time,
and the music would be there
even if the radio were not;
the radio simply allows us
to hear the music.

William Braden

A Useful Technique

There may be a real use for this recording technique after the subject
has been hypnotized several times.
Then it might be very useful from the
medical angle, when the subject is
being treated for, say, alcoholism or
stammering. The doctor might very
easily prepare a record for such a
subject, aimed at reinforcing and
repeating suggestions already given
in the hypnotic trance. Such a record
would, of course, be so arranged that
it would also awaken the subject
from the trance. This could very
easily be arranged and would be a
great convenience to both subject
and doctor.

G. H. Estabrooks

A Few Tiny Adjustments

It may be that a few tiny adjustments
if we knew how to make them would
open up the potentialities of genius
for every child.

David Dietz

An alternative way of reaching altered states of consciousness, that is not directly self-induced and yet does not involve a guide, is to use a tape recorder. The technique is simple and has often been suggested in works on self-hypnosis. The subject records beforehand the exercise he wishes to perform. Then, when he is ready to perform the exercise, he plays the recording back to himself and listens as if it were someone else speaking to him. A sample of trance induction suggestions for recording is offered on page 54.

As a person finds greater facility in reaching altered states of consciousness he will probably find that he becomes less and less dependent on the tape recording, simply by a process of automatic memorization. If, however, he is very dependent on hearing suggestions aloud, a recorded key word or phrase will eventually be all that he requires.

Learning

It takes discipline and practice to train mind and body to work together in harmony and to learn the skills involved in reaching altered states of consciousness. But, though it may be hard work, you will find many rewarding and encouraging signs of growth and development along the way. Each successive level of ability attained remains as a permanent possession. Everything learned is something that raises you to a higher plateau. Consequently, the preliminary skills of *Passages*— relaxation, concentration, counting down, entering into deeper and deeper states of consciousness—gradually become a part of your personality. In the beginning it may take you fifteen minutes or more to relax your body, but once physical relaxation—muscular equilibrium—becomes part of your daily living, the ability to relax becomes almost instantaneous. Gradually you will find yourself spending less and less time on the preliminaries, and more and more time on the fuller enjoyment of the parts of the exercises that influence your daily life.

A Return to Our Roots

Education toward the goal of individuality must cope with the difficulty of trying to prepare people for life's tasks with the least interference with their inherent nature, so that the desire for further growth can remain the motivating force throughout life. Repeatedly, in the different stages of life, patterns which once provided security have to be renounced so that new potentials can take their place. Since this cannot be brought about arbitrarily, it requires that time and again we return to our roots.

Magda Proskauer

A New Audacity

Every great advance
in science
has issued
from a new audacity
of imagination.

John Dewey

The Voyage Within

If a person can endure this voyage within his own experience, he can emerge from it with a new concept of his being and with new projects; the new concept of being will include more of his being in it. But this new integration will last only so long, and then the entire process must be repeated again. A sentient life is an endless series of getting out of one's mind and concepts, only to re-enter, and depart again.

Sidney M. Jourard

A success on His Planet

We've been assuming all along that failure was certain, that our universe was running down and it was strictly you or me, kill or be killed as long as it lasted. But now, in our century, we've discovered that man can be a success on his planet, and this is the great change that has come over our thinking.

R. Buckminster Fuller

Into a New Tongue

I am the poet of the Body and I am
    the poet of the Soul,
The pleasures of heaven are with me
    and the pains of hell are with me,
The first I graft and increase upon
    myself, the latter I translate into
    a new tongue.

Walt Whitman
Song of Myself

Advancing All Together

The outcome of the world, the gates
of the future, the entry into the super-
human—these are not thrown open
to a few of the privileged nor to one
chosen people to the exclusion of all
others. They will open to an advance
of all together, in a direction in which
all together can join and find com-
pletion in a spiritual renovation of
the earth.

Pierre Teilhard De Chardin

Pilgrims Together

Life is so full of meaning and purpose,
so full of beauty—beneath its cov-
ering—that you will find that earth
but cloaks your heaven. Courage,
then, to claim it—that is all. But
courage you have, and the knowledge
that we are pilgrims together, wend-
ing through unknown country, home.

Fra Giovanni

34

Getting There

Those who succeed in passing from one state of consciousness to another all have great difficulty in explaining exactly how they do it. In fact, some are quite unaware of what has happened, except that it has been an out-of-the-ordinary experience. *Passages* does not claim to present a series of techniques that work automatically. It does present techniques that will work with consistent practice. But they will work only for those who are prepared to enter into the experiences. *Passages* are sign posts to the right road, but it is up to the reader to go down that road.

Setting Out

There is but one state of mind from which you can "set out," namely, the very state of mind in which you actually find yourself at the time you do "set out" . . .

Charles Anders Peirce

A Journey toward Simplicity

Throughout history,
the way to understanding,
control and ecstasy
has been a long,
sinuous journey
toward simplicity
and unity.

George B. Leonard

Off on the Chase

The poet who embarks on the creation of the poem (as I know by experience), begins with the aimless sensation of a hunter about to embark on a night hunt through the remotest of forests. Unaccountable dread stirs in his heart . . . Then the poet is off on the chase. Delicate breezes chill the lenses of his eyes. The moon, curved like a horn of soft metal, calls in the silence of the topmost branches. White stags appear in the clearing between the tree trunks. Absolute night withdraws in a curtain of whispers. Water flickers in the reeds, quiet and deep . . .

García Lorca

Below the Threshold

The men who created the first European rationalism were never—until the Hellenistic Age—mere rationalists. They were deeply and imaginatively aware of the power, the wonder and the peril of the irrational. But they could describe what went on below the threshold of consciousness only in mythological or symbolic language; they had no instrument for understanding it, still less for controlling it . . . Modern man, on the other hand, is beginning to acquire such an instrument.

E. R. Dodd

The Human Tradition

Even now in the enthusiasm for new discoveries, reported public interviews with scientists tend to run increasingly toward a future replete with more inventions, stores of energy, babies in bottles, deadlier weapons. Relatively few have spoken of values, ethics, art, religion—all those intangible aspects of life which set the tone of a civilization and determine, in the end, whether it will be cruel or humane; whether, in other words, the modern world, so far as its interior spiritual life is concerned, will be stainless steel like its exterior, or display the rich fabric of genuine human experience. The very indifference of many scientists to such matters reveals how far man has already gone toward the world of the "outside," of no memory, of contempt toward all that makes up the human tradition.

Loren Eiseley

Preliminary Questions

A Third Way

We are here meeting a dimension of reality in the cosmos that is neither spiritualism nor materialism. It is a third way, a way of experiencing reality mediated by the depths of the psyche. It is just what it is, a roadway to reality through the deep psyche, and no metaphysical assumptions are necessary. Quite the contrary, when we have learned more about the modality of the symbolism that reflects the depths of the cosmos in man, we may have the information that will enable us to approach the ultimate and age-old questions of metaphysics in a new and wiser way.

Ira Progoff

What We Suppressed

Along with rediscovering our feelings and wants, is to recover our relation with the subconscious aspects of ourselves . . . As modern man has given up sovereignty over his body, so also he has surrendered the unconscious side of his personality, and it has become almost alien to him . . . we need to find and welcome back, so far as we can, what we suppressed.

Rollo May

The Pyramid of Memory

Our memories, at any given moment, form a solid whole, a pyramid, so to speak, whose point is inserted precisely into our present action. But behind the memories which are concerned in our present occupation and are revealed by means of it, there are others, thousands of others, stored below the scene illuminated by consciousness. Yes, I believe indeed that all our past life is there, preserved even to the most infinitesimal details, and that we forget nothing, and that all that we have felt, perceived, thought, willed, from the first awakening of our consciousness, survives indestructibly.

Henri Bergson

What is an altered state of consciousness?
An altered state of consciousness is any state of being which differs from our ordinary "rational" state of mind.

How does an altered state of consciousness differ from a hypnotic state?
The hypnotic states form a large part of the spectrum of altered states of consciousness, the latter being a more inclusive term. In *Passages* we are concerned with the various hypnotic states; however, since the term "hypnosis" still has many distorted negative connotations in America today, we prefer to use the general term "altered states of consciousness" to describe the trance states which, in many instances, could be conditions induced by hypnosis.

Are people able to self-induce an altered state of consciousness?
Yes. Spontaneous self-induced altered states of consciousness are quite common and you have probably experienced them many times yourself without knowing it. Whenever you become absorbed in anything, as in daydreaming, reading a book, or watching a television show, you may slip into an altered state of consciousness. During such times you are usually very relaxed, and oblivious of outside distractions. Self-induced altered states of consciousness are very common among artists and creative people in general.

How does the unconscious differ from ordinary consciousness?

The unconscious tends to accept as fact any idea that is presented to it. It is capable of thinking and reasoning but it does so in a different way from the conscious mind, in accordance with a different set of rules. It also can remember in complete and unselective detail, everything that has happened to the person, including events which the conscious mind has totally forgotten.

What is the relationship of altered states of consciousness to the unconscious?

Many feel that an altered state of consciousness is a condition which allows the subject to reach his unconscious or "inner mind" and influence it. Others feel that it provides an opening into a wider psychological or spiritual dimension, transcending the limits of the individual's unconscious.

How does an altered state of consciousness feel?

The altered states of consciousness described in *Passages* can be broadly classified as light, medium, and deep. In the first two there are few specific sensations other than feelings of great relaxation. In their early practice sessions with *Passages*, subjects may be surprised or disappointed because they don't feel any different. This is normal, and the best advice is to enjoy your sense of relaxation. Later, as you reach deeper states of altered consciousness, you will learn to determine and experience the depths of this feeling.

Does a person in an altered state of consciousness lose self-control?

Just as many people think that a hypnotized person will carry out any suggestion given to him, people also fear that they will lose control of themselves in an altered state of consciousness.

This is totally untrue. One will rarely do anything in an altered state of consciousness that he would not be ordinarily willing to do. Suggestions given to a person in an altered state of consciousness, whether by himself or by someone else, must be acceptable to both the conscious and unconscious parts of the mind.

The Question That Should be Asked

Can a person by hypnotized against his will? That, to a hypnotist, is a silly question. No psychologist who regarded himself as an authority in this field would waste his time trying to do so. He would use the disguised technique, a device well known to the research hypnotist, a device as successful as any other means of producing hypnotism. The question that should be asked is, "Can a man be hypnotized without his consent?" The answer is an emphatic "Yes."

G. H. Estabrooks

A Single Reality

As a result of my experiences, I believe that I exist not only in the familiar world of space and time, but also in a realm having a timeless, eternal quality. Behind the apparent multiplicity of things in the world of science and common sense, there is a single reality in which all things are united. (For example, it seems quite possible for people to communicate telepathically, without any use of sight or hearing, since deep down our minds are all connected anyway.)

Subject's evaluation
from Willis W. Harman
The Psychedelic Experience

Can an altered state of consciousness totally block out all attention to things that happen in normal life?
Yes—if the subject specifically wants to. However, people in altered states usually are aware of everything that goes on around them; they are merely so relaxed that they do not pay attention to anything except the matter they are focusing on.

How do self-induced altered states of consciousness differ from altered states of consciousness induced by such drugs as LSD, mescaline, or other hallucinogenic drugs?
The key word here is self-determination:

Subject matter. Usually no one can predict the trip on which an LSD subject will be taken. The outcome or effects of the trip may be good or bad—no one really knows beforehand. The subject of a self-induced altered state of consciousness can determine, sometimes in minute detail, the route of his trip.

Duration. The person under the influence of LSD normally remains in that state for many hours. A self-induced altered state of consciousness lasts just as long as the subject wishes it to last. This may mean anything from five minutes to five days.

Both Inside and Outside

It seems that absolutely everything
both inside and outside me
is happening by itself,
yet at the same time
that I myself am doing all of it,
that my separate individuality
is simply a function,
something being done
by everything which is not me,
yet at the same time
everything which is not me
is a function
of my separate individuality.

Alan Watts

The Search for Experience

Among the "insight" group of users,
many search for personal meditative,
religious, or mystic experiences.
Others of the same group
use LSD and other such psychedelics
to try and study the operations
and possibilities of their minds.
Once again, some say that this use
has led to a greater control
over the mental processes.
Others contend that it can lead
to loss of control,
often leaving a permanent
negative mark on the
individual personality.
The use of LSD can also apparently
alter the personality itself.

**Student Committee on Mental Health
Princeton University**

What kind of people make good subjects for altered states of consciousness?
It is the consensus of professional opinion that about 90% of the population can achieve an altered state of consciousness, and that approximately a third of them can enter deep states of alteration. Some experts feel that even this optimistic estimate is too conservative. Within the set of good subjects for altered states of consciousness there are many variants. These are discussed at appropriate places throughout the text.

Who should use altered states of consciousness?
The exercises in this book are perfectly safe—and decidedly helpful—for the vast majority of people. People who are very disturbed, emo-

40

tionally unsettled, or depressed should not use any self-help techniques that deal with the subconscious, especially in trying to solve their problems. Such persons should seek professional psychological or psychiatric help.

Does a person in an altered state of consciousness lose consciousness?
A subject in the type of trance states dealt with in this book never loses consciousness, even in the deeper stages. He knows what is happening around him at all times. He can talk and even walk while still remaining in an altered state of consciousness. However, there are very deep states in which the person experiences such intense bliss or ecstasy that it would be unwise for a person in such a state to attempt, for example, to drive a car.

Can you awaken yourself from a self-induced altered state of consciousness?
As was stated before, subjects in a self-induced altered state of consciousness are perfectly aware of what is happening around them and can awaken themselves at any time. Exercises given in *Passages* usually suggest a short ritual to bring the subject back to normal consciousness. The purpose of this ritual is twofold: (1) to provide a normal patterned passage back into ordinary consciousness, which eventually becomes natural and habitual, and (2) to ensure that the person return to ordinary consciousness in an alert and happy state. Thus, the passage back into ordinary consciousness involves bringing along some of the positive feelings experienced in the altered state of consciousness.

Is it better to self-induce an altered state of consciousness than to have someone else hypnotize you?
Yes, especially if the hypnotist is not a professionally trained person. In fact, you should *never* let anyone except a reliable and competent professional induce an altered state of consciousness in you. Self-induced states, however, tend to be entirely safe.

Points of View

Our time has been distinguished, more than by anything else, by a drive to control the external world,... and by an almost total forgetfulness of the internal world. If one estimates human evolution from the point of view of knowledge of the external world, then we are in many respects progressing.

If our estimate is from the point of view of the internal world and of oneness of internal and external, then the judgement must be very different.

R. D. Laing

Hidden in My Interior

I am fully aware of the fact that the mental state I am in has nothing to do with my usual mental state. I am no more the same man; I do not see or feel in the same way as before. I feel I have a double personality or, rather, as if one other person hidden in my deeper interior had suddenly emerged and replaced my normal personality. But yet, it does not seem to me that my usual thinking is entirely destroyed; this is certainly not the case. But beneath the surface of my conscious intelligence which directs my usual life, I feel there lives and works a subconscious intelligence, which is faster and more comprehensive than this one . . .

de Fleuriere

The Need for Wisdom

The world is now flooded with yogic teaching. Some of it is valid; much of it is half-baked, distorted, and otherwise corrupt; and some of it is demonic. Yoga is a powerful means to the greatest of all ends, but like all powerful things it is dangerous, and you can hurt yourself, nay, you can ruin yourself with it if you do not exercise wisdom.

The Gospel of Sri Ramakrishna

Slowly with Practice

The mind is like
a drunken monkey
that has just been
bitten by a scorpion

an undisciplined child
that you have let
run wild.

Slowly with practice
patience
you can teach this child
how to pin point
think/act
the way you
want/will it to.

Bernard Gunther

Decisions

There are those who know
gates are for closing and so close
every gate, often leaving life
shut off from the spring
to die of thirst.

There are those who know
Gates are for opening,
leaving the life
the gate was guarding
vulnerable to destruction.

There are those who know
gates are the pauses in the pulsing,
who listen to the rhythm
and move in con-sequence.

Ione Hill

Is it easier to return to an altered state of consciousness once you have been there?
Unquestionably, yes. Passing from ordinary states of consciousness into altered states is a technique which, with some practice, can be employed almost automatically, like a habit. Just as a musician finds it easier to play a difficult piece after much practice, so the person who practices reaching an altered state of consciousness finds it easier to enter that state each time he practices it.

How can a person practice the exercises in Passages without a guide? For example, how can I read the text of the exercise if my eyes are supposed to be closed?
It is suggested that you read through the exercise completely, becoming familiar with the details, before actually practicing it in an altered state of consciousness. However, if in the beginning you forget some details while in an altered state, you can include those the next time you practice the exercise. Once you have gained some facility, you can also open your eyes while in trance, and re-read the exercise in that state.

How can I learn to self-induce an altered state of consciousness?
By following the step-by-step directions given in the *Passages* exercises.

How long will it take me to learn to self-induce an altered state of consciousness?
Conscientious use of the techniques given in *Passages* should bring excellent results. Don't be discouraged if your efforts fail at first. Keep practicing and you will improve with each session. The unconscious likes repetition and ritual. By continued repetition, you will eventually reach an altered state of consciousness.

Will I continue to reach deeper and deeper levels of consciousness?
Your first experience of an altered state of consciousness may come after three or four tries

(though often it takes much longer), after which you will reach successively deeper states during the next five or six successful sessions. Then you will probably have arrived at your plateau of trance depth, which tends to remain stationary for a considerable period. If you are deeply involved and dedicated, you will experience further breakthroughs into still deeper levels at a later date. For most of the exercises in *Passages* a very deep state of trance is not required. For many purposes, in fact, the light and medium conditions are distinctly preferable since, in experienced subjects, very deep states tend to deteriorate into apathy.

Is sleep an altered state of consciousness?
Yes. Sleep is a different type of altered consciousness than those used in *Passages*. In the altered states utilized in *Passages*, you are emphatically *not* asleep and are completely aware of yourself and your surroundings.

What if I am pessimistic about my ability to self-induce an altered state of consciousness?
Doubts have a damaging effect. They can cause us to give up too soon, or they can make us try too hard, thereby working counter to the necessary relaxation. Set aside your doubts and focus on the idea of success. Also, forget all strain and effort, and simply *allow* yourself to relax.

Does time pass quickly in an altered state of consciousness?
Usually, yes. Your inner mind has its own sense of time. In fact, a half hour can seem like a few moments in an altered state of consciousness. There are exceptions, however, and some people find that time passes very slowly during altered consciousness.

Won't the preparation for entering the trance state simply put me to sleep?
Normally not. However, if you are very tired, you may pass from an altered state directly into normal sleep. This, however, can usually be prevented by suggesting to yourself that you will not fall asleep.

In and Out of Trance

After a little practice, a hypnotist can train a subject to go into the trance in literally one second, and to come out of it in the same time. The hypnotist would also remove from the subject all knowledge of having been hypnotized. If questioned on the matter, the subject would maintain that he had no interest whatsoever in hypnotism and had never been hypnotized in his life. This may seem hard to believe, but it is a mere chore to the practiced psychologist. Then he would probably make it impossible for anyone else to hypnotize the subject unless he, the operator, gave his consent—again, a little hard for the layman to believe, but a mere chore to the practitioner.

G. H. Estabrooks

Among Whirlpools

a boat, a stranger's boat, a canoe

and myself inside it, a stranger inside it

it floats past trees, past water

runs among whirlpools

Gitksan Indian Song

A Normal State

Sleep is a normal state, probably an essential period of rest for the entire nervous system, and yet it is also a state in which there is so much paranormal activity that it has always attracted the attention of the psychical researcher.

Alan Angoff

Time's Relativity

When you sit with a nice girl for two hours you think it's only a minute. But when you sit on a hot stove for a minute you think it's two hours. That's relativity.

Albert Einstein

The Focus of Motivation

Hypnotism has a startling capacity to step up motivation in the human being, to step up his motor, his driving power. In many cases, the human being is a failure because like Don Quixote he jumps on his horse and rides off madly in all directions at the same time. He does not channel his energy. With hypnotism, we can set up what we term a monomotivational field, wherein the energies of the individual are firmly pointed in one certain direction, with the exclusion of side issues and distractions.

G. H. Estabrooks

A Different Kind of Time

To begin with, this world has a different kind of time. It is the time of biological rhythm, not of the clock and all that goes with the clock. There is no hurry. Our sense of time is notoriously subjective and thus dependent upon the quality of our attention, whether of interest or boredom, and upon the alignment of our behavior in terms of routines, goals, and deadlines. Here the present is self-sufficient, but it is not a static present—the unfolding of a pattern which has no specific destination in the future but is simply its own point. It leaves and arrives simultaneously, and the seed is as much the goal as the flower. There is therefore time to perceive every detail of the movement with infinitely greater richness of articulation.

Alan Watts

Will I ever be able simply to slip into an altered state of consciousness in a few minutes?
After continuous practice one becomes proficient at self-induction. You can accelerate the process by suggesting to yourself, at each session, that you will remember the pathway to the altered state of consciousness and be able to find it more easily the next time. Experts in self-hypnosis can enter these states almost instantaneously—frequently by means of key symbols, which will be explained later.

What is the best preparation for reaching an altered state of consciousness?
The text of *Passages* gives specific directions for each exercise. In addition, these general suggestions will prove helpful:

(1) It makes no difference whether you sit up or lie down, but be sure you are *comfortable,* and that your clothing does not hamper or confine you.

(2) Learn to *relax.* Deep breathing helps to relax. The more you relax, the more comfortable you are, the easier it is for you to move into an altered state of consciousness. It will not do any harm to practice throughout the day.

How does self-suggestion work?
The golden key to successful suggestion and self-suggestion is *repetition.* In addition, keep the following points in mind:

1) Always word your suggestions positively. Don't say, "I will not hate that person," but "I will love that person."

2) You can address your unconscious in either the first or the second person, or you can switch from one to the other; but make suggestions—don't issue orders. Commands tend to set up automatic resistances, even when given by yourself to yourself. This may seem strange—but even when addressing your own mind, a phrase like "if you wish" will do wonders to oil the machinery.

3) Give your mind time to respond. Don't say, "When I open my eyes, my headache will be gone"; say, "When I open my eyes, my headache will begin to recede, and will continue to recede until it is gone."

4) Use short, simple, declarative sentences, and avoid ambiguities; the unconscious tends to be very literal-minded. Simple phrases will also be easier to remember from one session to the next, enabling you to repeat them, as far as possible, verbatim.

5) Don't overload the circuits! No matter how many problems you have, your inner mind can cope with them—one by one. At least in the beginning, don't work on more than two projects during any one session.

How will the inner mind carry out my suggestion? Your inner mind knows the best way, so let it take the initiative. In fact, you may find it worthwhile to encourage such initiative, by suggesting that your mind will approach or solve a problem in an *unexpected* way. This will lend your suggestion the additional spur of anticipation.

Is it best to schedule regular times for practicing the exercises in Passages? Yes. Set yourself a schedule for your *Passages* exercises and stick to it. You may find yourself putting sessions off or deciding that it's too much trouble. This is really resistance coming from your inner mind, which is not used to working in this way and naturally resists it. Perhaps you can use certain techniques within altered states of consciousness to find out why your inner mind is resisting.

What has an altered state of consciousness to do with better health? It is the unconscious mind that holds the ideas and attitudes that erupt in psychologically-caused illnesses. In an altered state of consciousness we can (1) learn what these ideas and attitudes are and (2) influence our inner minds to accept new ideas and attitudes leading to better mental and physical health.

The Support of Suggestion

Suggestion is of particular value when it is a present-day difficulty which is causing the anxiety, depression or sleeplessness, and which the patient finds himself incapable of dealing with. He needs support, and suggestion provides the temporary splint to tide him over the difficulty till he can carry on for himself.

J. A. Hadfield

A New Feeling

Carol sat in the lotus position. Legs intertwined, spine erect, hands forming circles resting on her knees. Eyelids half-mast, her gaze rested on the floor several feet in front of her. Gradually her breathing became more regular; the thoughts racing through her mind slowed; and a soft smile dawned on her face.

Eleanor Criswell

The Principle of Balance

No part of the body works alone—no organ, no function, no constituent element of blood, bone, or fiber works by itself or for itself alone. Balance plays through the whole. The simplest movement of a finger involves, we are told, sixty muscle-impulses—sixty unconscious shiftings to maintain oppositional balance—and the movement of the leg in walking, three hundred.

The complexity of muscle movement that these figures stand for need not blind us to the simplicity of the truth they stand for—that if even one of two impulses in an instrument constructed to work by the principle of balance is for any reason impaired, the balance between them is not merely impaired, it is destroyed—since balance either is, or is not.

Jennette Lee

Suggestion and Suggestibility

Suggestion **is the process of transmission and acceptance of an idea:** suggestibility **is the state of mind which makes such acceptance possible.**

J. A. Hadfield

A Positive Attitude

Never be negative . . . The ideal during meditation is to make the mind positive towards all outside interference, whether of intruding thoughts or actual entities, and yet be receptive to all higher influence coming from within. A little practice in this exercise will enable the student to achieve a happy combination of resistance and non-resistance, of positive and negative, in which all outside influence will be excluded, and yet the channels of inspiration be fully opened to the light within.

Christmas Humphreys

Two Original Forces

In human shape, in the mind-body, made of earth-stuff, we glimpse two original forces still at play: the body seeking to hold what it has achieved, the mind forever fleeing embodiment, seeking to realize in more significant form its visions. The body holds fast its automatic functioning—the bodily processes of breathing, digestion and assimilation of food, all that it has inherited from the past. The mind seeks to invent and enjoy new ways of life, experiments in existence for which the body has no taste.

Jennette Lee

What is a psychosomatic illness?
In general, illness springs from one of two causes. It may be entirely physical in origin or it may be psychosomatic, that is, a physical illness with psychological or emotional causes. This latter type of illness is the one that suggestion in an altered state of consciousness can help us overcome. (Many physicians now claim that over half of all illnesses fall into the category of psychosomatic.)

What are suggestions?
Suggestions are the phrases you say while in an altered state of consciousness to influence your inner mind. Usually these suggestions are repeated many times.

Can altered states of consciousness be used to remove pain?
Suggestions given in an altered state of consciousness are not magic or panacea but they can be effective tools in preserving and restoring your physical and mental health. An aspirin, for example, can relieve a headache but it doesn't remove the cause of the headache. Similarly, an altered state of consciousness can be utilized to remove the pain, but does not cure the cause of pain.

Can altered states of consciousness help me reduce tensions in my life?
Yes. Merely being in an altered state of consciousness can make you feel more relaxed than you ever were before. While in an altered state of consciousness you can suggest to yourself that the relaxed feeling will carry over into your ordinary consciousness. Suggest to yourself that you will be able to see your problems and challenges in a more and more productive way. Confidence in yourself and in solving problems also helps, naturally, to decrease tension.

Can altered states of consciousness reduce chronic fatigue?
Yes. Fatigue is often linked with tension; while in an altered state of consciousness you can suggest to yourself that the causes of fatigue in your life—tension, fear, conflict, worry, lack of proper motivation—need not influence you any longer.

Can altered states of consciousness help me overcome habits I want to get rid of?
Yes. Specific exercises in *Passages* are designed for that very purpose.

Are altered states of consciousness merely a practical tool, for example, for overcoming pain, relieving tension, losing weight?
No. As you use the exercises in *Passages* you are learning to think in a new way, learning to explore and discover many latent powers. Gradually looking at yourself while in an altered state of consciousness will become an important part of your life, by enhancing the quality of your life experiences.

Do the exercises follow a pattern or structure?
In each case (1) the goal of the exercise is clearly stated, as well as (2) the approximate time the exercise will take to complete. Then, (3) an induction technique is suggested to reach an altered state of consciousness, and (4) the details of the exercise itself are given. (5) A procedure for returning to ordinary consciousness is provided.

Psychologically, how does Passages work?
In general, the exercises in *Passages* help *all* of your body and its powers work together with *all* of your mind. Right now, possibly, because of tension, conflict, and fears, your body is working under emergency conditions utilizing only a fraction of your strength, and perhaps even operating against the wishes of your mind. Right now, too, because of mental stagnation, boredom, loneliness, unhappiness, or lack of self-confidence, your mind is working under extreme pressure conditions and utilizing only a fraction of its powers.

Passages provides a psychological way, without drugs or other artificial aids, of reaching altered states of consciousness. In these altered states of consciousness you begin to see things in a new way.

One by one, you can remove the causes keeping you from living a fully integrated life, with all the powers of mind-body working in harmony and to their fullest capacities.

The Body Knows How

All awkward movements of the body, distorted gestures, and the attitudes and postures . . . come from self-conscious handling of the body. The body knows how to do what it is told, with beauty and strength, if the mind will stop trying to help or coerce it and will keep to its own part in the functional process—seeing clearly what is to be done, telling the body to do it, and leaving it alone to do it in its own way—which means withdrawing false tensions and misconceptions and letting it function in synergetic wholeness.

Jennette Lee

Seeing Goes Beyond

We never see only what we see;
we always see something else
with it and through it!
Seeing creates, seeing unites,
and above all
seeing goes beyond itself.

Paul Tillich

To Move Beyond Drugs

Believing as I do
that both the individual
and the society are giving
far too much attention
to mind-altering drugs
and that, for the society as a whole,
the more people depend
on such drugs,
the less likely they are
to involve themselves
in creative social change,
it is important to move the society
beyond drugs.

Joel Fort

BEING

1. Trance Induction Methods

And the Fall was Over

Down, down, down. There was nothing else to do, so Alice soon began talking again. 'Dinah'll miss me very much to-night, I should think!' (Dinah was the cat.) 'I hope they'll remember her saucer of milk at tea-time. Dinah, my dear! I wish you were down here with Me! There are no mice in the air, I'm afraid, but you might catch a bat, and that's very like a mouse, you know. But do cats eat bats, I wonder?' And here Alice began to get rather sleepy, and went on saying to herself, in a dreamy sort of way, 'Do cats eat bats? Do cats eat bats?' and sometimes 'Do bats eat cats?' for, you see, as she couldn't answer either question, it didn't much matter which way she put it. She felt that she was dozing off, and had just begun to dream that she was walking hand in hand with Dinah, and was saying to her, very earnestly, 'Now, Dinah, tell me the truth: did you ever eat a bat?' when suddenly, thump! thump! down she came upon a heap of sticks and dry leaves, and the fall was over.

Lewis Carroll

There are many pathways into altered states of consciousness. All of them can be used interchangeably, either singly or in combination, according to one's mood at the time. The methods are usually classified as follows:

Relaxation (physical and mental)
Sensory deprivation
Sensory overload
Restriction of motion
Disturbance of equilibrium
Eye fixation

Another means of speeding the induction is to roll your eyes upward, either behind your already closed lids or before closing them.

You can also establish a key phrase and image for returning to the reality state. This might be, for example, an image of yourself pushing off from the bottom of a deep pool, rising slowly to the count of one to three, and breaking surface at three.

Everybody should expect off days; at times the altered state eludes even the most expert. When you run into such a block don't fight it; turn to something else. Keep your success pattern intact and try again another day. On the other hand, even though you seem to be experiencing a poor day, don't give up too quickly; sometimes you just need a little more coaxing than usual. Try some soft, relaxing music to help create a more receptive mood.

These are general guidelines. You will develop your own techniques as you go along. For the moment, just remember that an altered state of consciousness is as natural to the human mind as sleep or the ordinary waking state. No matter how difficult reaching the altered state may seem during the first attempts, you are certain to reach it in time, with patience and practice.

The Ready Subconscious

The first thing I do when I am conscious of the coming of a poem is to seek paper and pencil. It seems as though the simple gazing at a piece of blank paper hypnotizes me into an awareness of the subconscious . . . This state of semi-trance is not surprising when we think of short poems; what is curious is that the trancelike state can hold over interruptions in the case of long poems. When a poem is so long that days or weeks are needed to write it, the mere sitting down to continue it produces the requisite frame of mind, which holds (except for the lacunae **I have spoken of) throughout its correction. On the other hand, no power will induce it if the subconscious is not ready.**

Amy Lowell

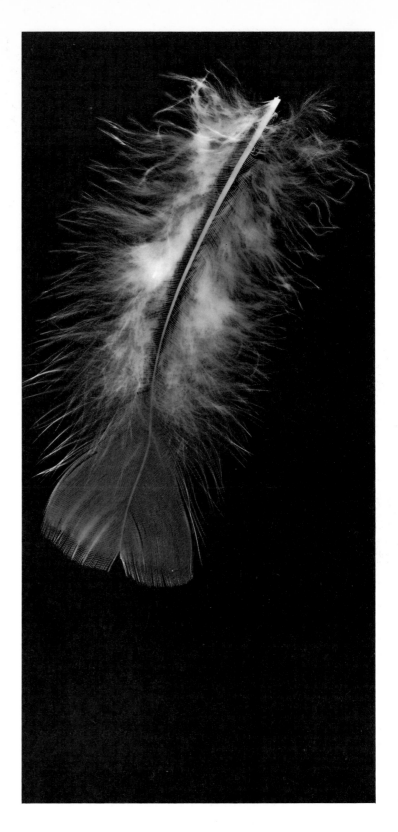

Creating a Receptive State

With the instrumentation now available, it is not only possible to evolve new states of consciousness by controlling a variety of internal parameters, but one can also help people attain states that have been known to Zen and yoga practitioners for centuries. By studying these practitioners with physiological recording techniques, we can determine what aspects of their physiology they alter to attain these states. One can then begin to train people to control a number of specific functions that were found to be altered . . . a crude attempt to enable Western man to place his physiology in a receptive state that will more easily allow his psychology to be altered.

Richard Davidson
and Stanley Krippner

In *Passages,* relaxation techniques are stressed, because they constitute the easiest and safest method of self-induction.

Throughout the text a variety of different relaxation methods are offered to accommodate individual preferences. After some practice and experience, your favorite and most successful methods will emerge. For example, most people instinctively choose a relaxation technique that involves downward movement (floating down, going down a staircase, riding down an elevator). Others, however, equally instinctively adopt images denoting upward movement (floating up, riding up an escalator, drifting upward in a balloon). Neither is superior to the other; the best method for you is the one you find most congenial and most effective.

At the outset of your mental journeys you may find the learning of simple physical relaxation more difficult than you expected. Once physical relaxation is mastered, however, mental relaxation follows easily and naturally.

The crux of relaxation-induction is repetition—repetition intensified by motivation. Never allow an induction ritual to become meaningless through sheer monotony. By-rote mumbling without the elan of motivation will only lead to frustration. When using any relaxation technique, speak to yourself very slowly, in simple phrases, allowing the words and images to become even more effective through repetition; and let the repeated words and images acquire an emotional coloration through a sense of familiarity and anticipation of success.

Besides using the count from ten to zero, you should also use some key phrases and images to help you across the threshold—phrases such as "relax now" or "deeper and deeper," and images such as yourself riding down an escalator or floating down an enclosed winding staircase. One way to set up such key symbols is to tell yourself, during a particularly successful induction, that henceforth a certain phrase—for example, "deeper and deeper"—will always herald a deeper level of consciousness. To make this assurance doubly effective, you may combine the phrase and the image: Hear yourself repeating the phrase "deeper and deeper" while seeing yourself riding down an escalator.

Sensory Awakening

No urging can bring anyone to faster sensations; on the contrary, it would only block experiencing. At first, lying on the floor may help bring quiet, for nearly everybody likes to lie down and with that gains a feeling of comfort which facilitates sensory awakening. Of course, some people who are particularly restless may feel this is indulgence and become uneasy. Others who have always equated consciousness with activity will become drowsy. But gradually they recognize that peace can bring gradual clearing of the head rather than drowsiness and that giving time as needed is essential for the development of quiet alertness.

Charlotte Selver

A Most Extraordinary Activity

The body may be passive, resting in this supine position, but this is the most extraordinary activity that goes on. How can I describe it to you? It's so mysterious, this creative act. No one has really ever described it well. I think Thomas Mann came pretty close to it in Dr. Faustus, but that was under such extraordinary conditions that it doesn't apply to everybody. The creative act, if it's really creative, is something that seizes you, and it is active. It is passive only in the sense that you are somehow a slave of it. In other words, this compulsion causes you to be passive only in the sense that you are in the clutches of something.

Leonard Bernstein

2. Model Induction Talk

The Whole Outlook Changed

I came back into the hall and was about to go to my seat when the whole outlook changed. A broad expanse opened, and the ground appeared as if all caved in . . . As I looked around and up and down the whole universe with its multitudinous sense-objects now appeared quite different; what was loathsome before, together with ignorance and passions, was now seen to be nothing else but the outflow of my own inmost nature which in itself remained bright, true, and transparent.

Yuan-Chou

If after repeated attempts to self-induce an altered state of consciousness you have not yet been successful, then, on tape or cassette, using another's voice or your own, make a recording of the following induction talk. When recording, speak slowly and distinctly in a soothing voice, remembering to pause at the end of lines, between dots, and between paragraphs. Once you have recorded the induction talk, you can play it for yourself whenever you want to enter an altered state of consciousness. The recording will help your mind to develop a pattern for reaching altered states. Each time you use the talk you will be able to enter into a deeper state.

In a short time, you will have learned how to enter your altered states and will no longer need to use your induction recording.

Let your eyelids grow heavy easily,
very naturally,
growing heavier and heavier
as they have before . . .

Feel your whole body
beginning to grow very relaxed now,
just growing deeper,
and deeper, and deeper relaxed . . .
Deeper . . . and deeper . . . and deeper . . .
Your eyelids heavier . . .
and heavier . . . and heavier.

The entire body relaxing now,
mentally and physically,
from the top of the head
all the way down
to the very tips of the toes.
Just growing deeper . . . and deeper . . .
Relaxed . . . and more relaxed . . .
Deeper . . . and deeper . . . and deeper.

I am going to count slowly from ten to zero now,
and as I count backwards,
you will feel yourself going
into a still deeper trance;
and by the time I reach zero,
you will be much deeper than you are now,
very deeply, very pleasantly relaxed,
and in a very deep trance. (10, 9, 8, 7, 6 . . .)
Deeper and deeper and deeper,
still deeper . . .
very deeply now . . .

The entire body relaxing,
from head to toe, completely,
as you continue to go deeper and deeper,
deeper . . . and deeper relaxed . . .
Very deeply now.
And you can continue to go
still more deeply
with each passing moment,
completely at ease, deeply relaxed,
deeper . . . and deeper . . . and deeper . . .
Deeper . . . and deeper . . .

The Need for a New Framework

The Newtonian framework, as was natural after 250 years, had been found too crude to accommodate the new observational knowledge which was being acquired. In default of a better framework, it was still used, but definitions were strained to purposes for which they were never intended. We were in the position of a librarian whose books were still being arranged according to a subject scheme drawn up a hundred years ago, trying to find the right place for books on Hollywood, the Air Force, and detective novels.

Sir Arthur Eddington

Training for Control

For thousands of years Eastern mystics and yogis have demonstrated remarkable control over mind and body, while we Westerners have tended to dismiss them as charlatans when they were buried alive for hours, dropped their pulse to the vanishing point or demonstrated that they could listen during their sleep. However, today in the West a number of prestigious laboratory clinics are training people to control their heart rate, lower blood pressure, change skin temperature, relax certain muscles, or produce certain brain waves — and thus to control without drugs cardiac arrhythmias, symptoms of insomnia, migraine and tension headaches.

Gay Luce and Erik Peper

3.
Believing is Seeing

GOAL

To develop the ability of your mind's eye to visualize clearly and vividly.

Whatever your purpose in expanding your mind through *Passages*—greater happiness and self-fulfillment, increased insight, or enhanced creativity—the ability to visualize clearly and vividly is an invaluable asset. Indeed, for some forms of mind expansion it appears to be an essential prerequisite.

Native aptitude for visualization varies from individual to individual; but all of us can improve our ability by consistent practice.

As you get to know yourself and your response pattern, you will want to create your own variations on the following warm-up exercises, or give them a slightly different slant which serves your purpose better.

TIME

Approximately fifteen minutes.

PREPARATION

Choose a time and place in which you can be fairly sure of being undisturbed for, say, fifteen minutes. Close your eyes, and imagine yourself sitting in a dark room, in front of a large white screen. For a few moments, allow nothing to intrude on this empty, white expanse. The monotony of this expanse will gradually induce a light trance state.

THE EXERCISE

Now, in your mind's eye, create a picture of an empty glass and project it onto the screen. Be sure to visualize it on the *screen*, rather than behind your closed lids. (At least in the beginning, you should make a special effort to project visualized objects *outward*.)

When the image of the glass in your mind's eye

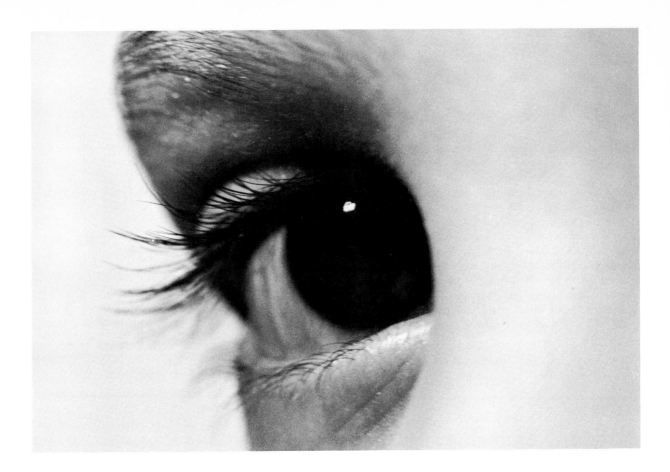

is as clear and three-dimensional as you can make it at this time, fill it with a strongly-tinted liquid, such as coffee or Coke. Now add some ice cubes. Next, provide a straw. Make it a colorful one—candy-striped, for example, or a solid primary color. Now add the caption 'Coffee' or 'Coke' underneath, in a variety of styles. First visualize it as typewritten, next as handwritten then as printed.

This process of creating pictures in your mind's eye should be repeated with other objects, of graduated complexity. When the ability to visualize individual objects has been mastered, proceed to scenes—an apartment (perhaps furnished in a variety of styles), a department store, a playground.

Lastly, practice visualizing individuals. This can be surprisingly tricky and frustrating, but here too steady, relaxed practice will bear fruit. You may find, for example, that you can easily picture a comparative stranger, whereas a far more familiar face consistently eludes you—especially

Finding All Faces Different

Consider human faces, for example. Anyone who takes a moment to think will realize the marvelous fact that human faces are, at the same time, very much alike and yet very different. Among the vast numbers of men and women on earth, every human face is like every other human face and there is no difficulty in distinguishing the human species from that of the rest of the animals. At the same time, every human face is unlike every other face and there is no difficulty in telling one person from another. We say that faces are all alike, and yet we find them all different. We should expect all faces to look alike, since all persons share the same human nature. Variety is the real surprise, finding all faces different.

Saint Augustine

Overlooking

Normally we do not
so much look at things
as overlook them.

Alan Watts

Selective Awareness

Through entering into a series of experiences designed to revitalize your
sense of smell, touch, and taste, you
can extend your horizon of awareness. Participation in experiences
designed to foster what has been
called sensory awakening can enhance your capacity for selective
awareness—so that you can open
yourself to awareness either at will
or spontaneously.

Herbert A. Otto

Watching from a Distance

I was watching a carnival from a distance, watching thousands of colored
balloons, little ones crammed into
huge ones, every color, all filled with
helium, when suddenly the balloons
broke loose and began floating up-
wards. There was a child hanging
from each big balloon, about three
children in all, and everyone
screamed, "Hang on," and I won-
dered how in hell they would get
those children down.

They floated over the land towards
the sea, and the balloons began
popping.

A huge carnival ride was pushed out
into the sea, and jets came over and
police cars were ready in the water
and children were tearing about
planning to catch the floaters when
they hit the water. I remember wondering if they wouldn't get smothered
under popped balloons before anyone could get to them. I think they
made it OK into a police car, down
a ramp of the carnival ride, into the
ocean and were towed through the
water to safety.

Joan Baez

when you try to get at the essence of the expression rather than contenting yourself with an
approximation.

It may help you to see such a "difficult" individual against a variety of backgrounds; certain
poses may prove less problematic than others.
For an especially elusive face it may help to sneak
up on it by visualizing the back of the head first,
then working your way around the profile, and
inching forward gently until the full frontal view
comes into focus.

Make use of whichever of your senses serves you
best. Most people are visually oriented, others
tend to feature sounds or the feel of things. Do
you have exceptionally good hearing? Then, in
developing your ability to grasp a person in your
mind, hear that person's mood in the innumerable inflections of his voice and in his choice of
words, while you visualize the expression in his
eyes, his posture and his gestures.

Is your sense of smell very acute? Perhaps recalling in your mind a whiff of a particular fragrance
will instantly evoke a face reluctant to appear.

The means you can use to achieve expertise are
as varied as human personality; and to find your
own most congenial method of visualizing an
object will in itself be a step toward enhanced
self-awareness.

4.
Lift-Off

To develop a technique for signaling the receptivity of your mind to self-suggestions. One indication of an altered state of consciousness is the raising of one's hand and arm by ideomotor activity (involuntary movement as a direct result of suggestion or ideational thought).

TIME
Approximately half an hour.

A WORD OF ADVICE

Ideomotor activity is a subject on which many half-truths have been disseminated and too widely accepted. It is often designated as one of the earliest signs of hypnotic trance. And many people do, in fact, achieve ideomotor activity in a very light trance state. Others, however, can achieve it only in deeper trance states. To some, it comes effortlessly at first try; others require long, concentrated practice. If you are among the latter group, don't give up, but keep trying, without anxiety. Sooner or later you will acquire the knack, and eventually you will reach the point of lift-off within a very few minutes.

PREPARATION

Lie in bed or on a sofa with your arms extended at your sides, or sit in a comfortable chair with your forearm and hands resting on the arms of the chair. Be sure all ten fingers touch the bed or chair. Fix your eyes on some focal point—a lamp, a picture, or even a crack in the wall—and continue to look at it as long as it is comfortable to do so. Then let your focus blur and let your eyes close and your body relax. Visualize the areas of your body as you coax successive muscle groups into letting go.

When your body is fully relaxed, tell yourself that you will now count slowly from ten down to zero and that, on reaching zero, you will be very relaxed, very deeply and pleasantly relaxed, more relaxed than ever before.

THE EXERCISE

When you have counted down to zero and have reached this deep state of relaxation, tell yourself that within a few moments you will feel a tingling sensation in one of your fingers. Wait calmly until the tingling begins. Maintain the relaxed state of equilibrium, so that you don't hinder the sensation from emerging by either excessive concentration or diffuse inattention. As soon as you become aware of the tingling, tell yourself that within a few seconds it will spread to all the fingers of that hand; then along the fingers to the knuckles, over the back and palm of the hand, all the way up to the wrist. Give your mind time to accept these suggestions, while you maintain an even trance level—like the idling motor of a car.

As soon as your mind has complied, and you feel the tingling all over the hand, tell yourself that

Cutting off the Feelings

Firmly planted in his loved or despised mind, our man is unaware that he is deliberately controlling his body. It is his body, with which he has certain external contacts, but it is not he; he does not feel himself.

Assume now, that he has many things to cry about. Every time he is stirred to the point of tears, he nevertheless does not "feel like crying," and he does not cry: this is because he has long habituated himself not to be aware of how he is muscularly inhibiting this function and cutting off the feeling—for long ago it led to being shamed and even beaten.

Instead, he now suffers headaches, shortness of breath, even sinusitis. (These are now more things to cry about.) The eye muscles, the throat, the diaphragm are immobilized to prevent the expression and awareness of the coming crying. But this self-twisting and self-choking in turn arouse excitations (of pain, irritation, or flight) that must in turn be blotted out, for a man has more important arts and sciences for his mind to be busy with than the art of life and the Delphic self-knowledge.

Paul Goodman

you will soon feel slight spasms in the tingling hand and that the hand itself will begin to lift off the surface on which it is resting. When you feel it beginning to lift, allow your hand and arm to lift at its own speed and of its own volition, neither helping nor hindering it. Let it rise as far as it wants to go: Observe the movement inside you (for your eyes are still closed) as your arm rises to its apex then remains there for some moments or even minutes, comfortably suspended in a position you could not maintain without strain in your ordinary state of awareness. And right here is your goal: proof positive of your altered state of consciousness.

While your arm is still in that position, tell yourself that from now on your entry into this particular state of mind will be expressed by the ideomotor activity of your raised hand. In subsequent exercises, it will indicate that your unconscious mind has reached a state of receptiveness and is prepared to accept and carry out the suggestions you give it.

Now wait for your hand to fall back of its own accord; or, if you wish, tell yourself that within a few seconds your hand will gently drop back into its original position. This can be done without disturbing the receptive state of your mind.

Remember also to implant a safeguard suggestion: Tell yourself that you will always awaken from this or any other altered state of consciousness by counting from one to three and then opening your eyes; and that, in case of emergency, you will awaken instantly and completely by simply opening your eyes. You will always awaken refreshed, relaxed, and fully alert.

Listen

If you are
in conflict
within your self
have the
different parts
talk out loud
to one another.

Listen
to what they
have to say
to each other.

Feel find out
what they/you
really want
to do.

Bernard Gunther

5. Twenty Questions

PREPARATION

If convenient, do the exercise lying down, to allow your hands and arms complete freedom of movement. Close your eyes, and feel yourself relaxing, from the top of your head to the tips of your toes, descending easily into a deeper and deeper level of mind.

THE EXERCISE

When you have achieved a trance state, suggest to yourself that your deeper mind will now choose one of your fingers to represent the answer "yes," by causing it to lift. At this point, deepen your trance a little, and wait until one of your fingers begins to tingle, and then to lift. It will probably tremble a little as it begins to rise, and it may rise just perceptibly or all the way to a pointing position. Either way, this finger now represents the answer "yes."

Repeat the same process, allowing your deeper mind to suggest another finger to represent "no," a third finger to represent "perhaps" or "I don't know," and a fourth one to represent "I don't want to answer."

If you prefer, you may also do the designating of fingers yourself—deciding, for instance, that the right index finger will represent "yes," the left one "no," etc.

GOAL
To question the subconscious mind by means of ideomotor (involuntary) finger movements.

TIME
About 15-20 minutes are required for this exercise.

Now, in simple and unambiguous terms, ask your subconscious a question to which your conscious mind does not know the answer, and await developments.

A good opening move is to ask a question with a checkable answer, such as, for example, the location of an item—a sweater, a pin, or a book—which you've put away so "carefully" that you've forgotten where it is.

Getting the first ideomotor response from your fingers may take time, and even when you have mastered this exercise, it is not a fool-proof technique. But its ratio of accuracy is high, and the technique will prove useful in many ways.

Should you ask a question and get a response which does not seem right, reword the question; it may have been phrased too ambiguously or too all-inclusively to allow a clear answer. Like most exercises, this one also requires practice and the development of skills—not the least of which is the ability to ask clear and direct questions.

NOTE

At the beginning, it is better to choose subjects which do not have great emotional significance for you, because it takes practice and discipline to keep your questioning self neutral, and to avoid conscious or unconscious attempts to influence the answer. Obviously, getting a response from the desired finger by concentrating on it, will elicit an answer based on wishful thinking rather than on the stored knowledge of the unconscious.

The Language of Symbols

Knowing that the knowledge which the deep psyche derives from its contact with the cosmos is transmitted in symbolic form, we must discipline ourselves not to take the messages of the deep psyche literally. When the information comes couched in imagery and is dramatized as a person, known or unknown to us, we are not to suppose that it is a soul entity that is appearing to us. This would be to interpret the deep psyche literally whereas its nature is to transmit its knowledge symbolically.

Ira Progoff

Another Automatic Technique

Automatic writing is a much more satisfactory technique because replies are not limited to yes **or** no. **The subconscious can even volunteer information. The late Anita Muhl, a psychiatrist, was undoubtedly our leading authority on automatic writing. She claimed that four out of five persons could learn to automate, although many would require long hours of training to succeed. Certainly some can learn this very quickly, but the percentage is not large. But almost any hypnotic subject capable of reaching the somnambulistic state will automate readily.**

Leslie LeCron

7.
On Stage

PREPARATION

Relax your whole body as completely as you can, beginning with the top of your head, your forehead, face, throat, chest, abdomen, legs, and feet. Count slowly from ten to zero, while mentally tracing the progress of your relaxation.

THE EXERCISE

GOAL
To develop self-confidence in talking to a group; and to learn to see the experience of publicly talking to others as a pleasurable one.

TIME
Set aside fifteen minutes daily for a week or so. The best times for doing the exercise are the period right after awakening, or, alternatively, the period just before falling asleep. In this sort of exercise, where an element of elation is useful, the time of highest bodily temperature (usually late afternoon) might also be considered.

Now you are completely relaxed, from the top of your head to the very tips of your toes. Imagine yourself standing on stage in a theater auditorium behind closed curtains, just before the start of your talk. The house lights are dimmed, and the noise in the audience quiets to an expectant hush. In your mind, count silently from one to three. When you have reached three, the curtain will open, and you will see yourself on stage, standing behind a lectern, dressed as you plan to be on the actual occasion. Behind you there is a screen, for the visual material you are planning to use to illustrate your talk.

Now focus on yourself on the stage. See your self-confident poise—just the right combination of formality and relaxation. A glass of water stands within reach of your left hand. The microphone is directly in front of you, and you welcome it as an extension of yourself, an added means of reaching out to your audience.

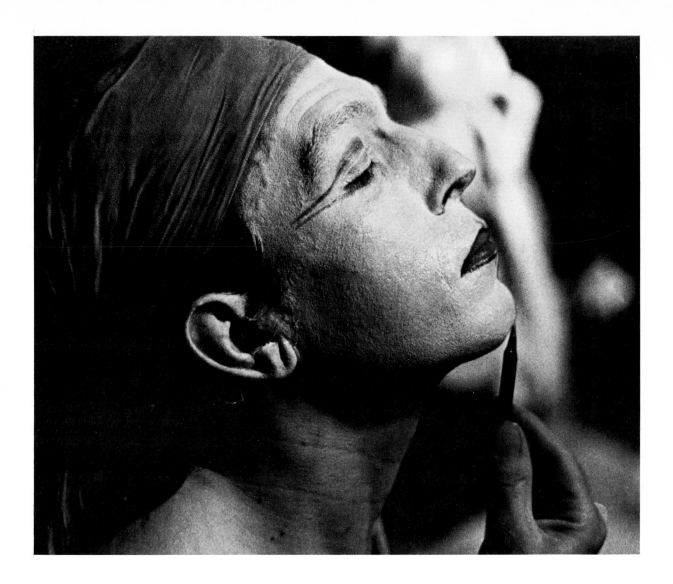

The manuscript with your speech rests on the lectern before you, but it is really no more than a prop. You see the pages with photographic recall, knowing exactly at which point each page ends and the next one begins. As you speak, you turn the pages at the appropriate moments, but it is not really necessary, because you see the manuscript clearly enough in your mind's eye to "read" it off.

You do this while you look straight out at your audience, at the many upturned faces reflecting friendliness, interest and close attention.

Once in a while you pause to take a sip of water, using the brief silence as a change of pace. Your voice needs neither rest nor lubrication. You can

Suffering and Growth

You don't have to suffer continual chaos in order to grow.

John C. Lilly

Self-confidence

By their behavior and own life style, in addition to what they communicate directly in the classroom, the teachers should seek to convey that it is possible and usually desirable to relate to others, and seek meaning, happiness, and achievement without alcohol, tobacco, marijuana, or the rest.

Joel Fort

hear how effective it is. It is perfectly clear, perfectly modulated, expressing your thoughts without any strain. You speak as if you were addressing some close friends in the familiarity of your own living room. There is no need for greater volume. The microphone does the extra work for you, carrying your words to the farthest corners of the auditorium, to all these people who think well enough of you to devote an evening of their time to you, who have come to hear what you have to say and to be stimulated by you.

And you know you are fulfilling your part of your contract with the audience. You know that you are doing your job well. You feel completely at ease, completely in tune with your environment.

NOTE

Repeat this sequence at least once a day for a week or so and, as always, strive for the most vivid visualization you are capable of. When the real occasion is at hand, it will lose whatever menace it may have had and will turn into a thoroughly enjoyable experience.

The Necessary Resources

Seeing who I really am, it is silly to ever feel basically inadequate, because anything I really need to do, I have the necessary resources for. There is no need to be fearful of the future; I now see that death, trouble and pain are not evils which one must be resigned to, but, rather, experiences which contribute to human growth. Whereas I may have once thought that people could hurt my feelings, or make me angry, resentful or bitter, or cause me embarrassment, I now see that in a very real sense no one can hurt me unless I let him.

> **Subject's evaluation**
> **from Willis W. Harman**
> **The Psychedelic Experience**

8.
Somewhere Time

GOAL:

To give up smoking by means of time distortion. Setting aside mechanical aids such as nausea-inducing drugs, which are outside the province of this book, you have two alternative ways of dealing with the problem: The "cold turkey" approach of giving up all forms of tobacco at once, for good; or the method of cutting down gradually, over a period ranging from several days to a couple of weeks.

The approach you choose will depend on your personality and previous experience with breaking habits. Time distortion, properly used, can greatly assist either method. This exercise presumes that your approach is to cut down gradually.

Let us assume that you have reached a new plateau in your cutting down process and are now limiting yourself to one cigarette in the morning, one at midday, and one at night. Smoking still has a great hold on you, and you find the period between the morning and midday cigarettes interminable. Why not speed it up?

INTRODUCTORY NOTE

One of mankind's oldest clichés speaks of hours that seem like minutes, or minutes that seem like hours. You are, the saying implies, at the mercy of time. What is true, in fact, is that you are held fast by your emotions of eagerness or dread, by joyous or apprehensive anticipation.

But you do not have to be. Just as your mind can surmount the barrier of confinement in space and liberate you, so it can jump the hurdle of minutes and hours. This technique is called time distortion. By means of it you can speed up or slow down your perception of time, to suit your purposes or your emotional needs.

The areas of application are vast, ranging from the strictly practical to the highly spiritual. In this first exercise we will work toward a practical goal. You will then be able to adapt it to your own needs.

PREPARATION

Put yourself into your altered state of consciousness with your eyes open, by fixing your eyes on a page of fairly small print until the lines blur.

Fern Hill

Time held me green and dying
Though I sang in my chains like the
sea.

Dylan Thomas

The Passage of Time

While the hands of a clock move from
one position to another, an infinite
number of other changes take place
in the cosmos. And wherever that
phenomenon which we call awareness exists, there is probably a sense
of the passage of time, and a sense of
sequence. In other words, experience
seems to be inseparably interwoven
with time sense which, as is true of
other 'primary' experience, is inde-
finable. Yet we all know what it is,
and we apparently conceive of duration as a magnitude, for we speak of a
long or short time, and readily compare time intervals one with another.
Our experience of time differs from
that of space in a strange way in that
it seems to be of us, and inseparable
from our very existence.

Milton H. Erickson and Lynn F. Cooper

THE EXERCISE

With your eyes open, tell yourself that you will now count from ten to zero, and that, on reaching zero, you will become wholly absorbed by the task which you are at this time supposed to perform.

Suggest to yourself, in addition, that this task or train of thought will absorb you for a specified length of time (until your next cigarette is due), beginning from the moment you have returned to your reality state by counting from one to three. When that period is over, tell yourself that you will look at your watch and be utterly amazed at the speed with which time has passed, and at the ease with which you have endured the period of deprivation.

If you are not working at a job, word your suggestion differently—to the effect that you will become totally absorbed in the tasks that are on your schedule for this particular period of day, or those that could profitably be done at this time.

NOTE

Once you have gained facility, you can set your mind harder tasks. The next exercise might be worded to include a period half an hour beyond the time of your next cigarette; after that, try for a delay of an hour, two hours, and so on.

Perform this exercise often, and lead your mind at a slow but even pace. Invite a self-perpetuating success rather than risking failure by reaching too far too fast.

This exercise has two clearly valuable effects: first, it eases the period of deprivation; second, it enables you to become totally absorbed in your work and not in the deprivation.

The Mind's Invention

Mind invented contradictions, invented names; it called some things beautiful, some ugly, some good, some bad. One part of life was called love, another murder. How young, foolish, comical this mind was. One of its inventions was time. A subtle invention, a refined instrument for torturing the self even more keenly and making the world multiplex and difficult. For then man was separated from all he craved only by time, by time alone, this crazy invention! It was one of the props, one of the crutches that you had to let go, that one above all, if you wanted to be free.

Hermann Hesse
Klein and Wagner

A Relativity Limerick

There was a young lady called Bright
Whose speed was much faster than light
She went out one day
In a relative way
And came back the previous night.

Arthur Butler

9.

Body Mirage

Study the accompanying photograph. Something seems odd, doesn't it? Because the faces appear behind a magnifying glass one expects them to be distorted, yet they are not.

No matter what the facts and reasons may be for picturing a thing in a certain way, your mind, like the magnifying glass, has the power to alter this image for your benefit. The following exercise describes only one of an almost infinite number of ways in which this exercise can benefit you.

Let us assume that you have gained an unwanted twenty pounds. Imperceptibly, as your figure has changed, your self-image has changed with it—so much so that by now you see yourself as almost deformed by the excess poundage, even though your "objective" mind knows that your appearance is not really so drastically changed.

PREPARATION

Put yourself into a medium trance by fixing your eyes on a point above eye-level, until they become sufficiently strained to close. Deepen your altered state of consciousness by suggestions of deeper and deeper relaxation.

GOAL
To modify your physical image of yourself by altering your way of looking at yourself.

TIME
Allow approximately 30 minutes.

78

THE EXERCISE

Picture yourself standing in front of a full-length mirror. You see yourself in your present, excess state. But as you keep looking at your mental mirror image, the outlines of your figure become a little blurred and your image recedes slightly. Focus on your blurred image, while maintaining or even deepening your trance.

Now your figure is very definitely receding within the mirror, and becoming slimmer the more distant it grows—as if it were receding not only in substance but also in time, to the period before the excess weight encumbered it.

Now the picture becomes much sharper and advances again. Focus all your attention on this new image of yourself, and while holding it firmly in your mind's eye, tell yourself that you will now slowly count from ten to zero. When

New Forms of Life

The end is, not to emancipate the spirit from the instrument it entered into at birth, but to fill it with the wonder and mystery of this inter-working of mind and body, and to learn from the wisdom and patience and strength that have built it up what is signified when it points to new forms of life.

Jennette Lee

A Sense of Lightness

One learns to visualize an inner body space, while simultaneously concentrating on one's exhalation, as if the breath were sent into that particular space. This may change the blood pressure and lead to a sense of lightness.

Magda Proskauer

you have reached zero, the slim mirror image will begin to move, spontaneously, and it will move with the grace and agility that goes with its slim shape.

Feel each of its movements in your own body— for this is, after all, your own body, *your* grace and agility, *your* slim shape. You feel each movement as your own, because they *are* all your own. This graceful agile you *is* you.

Watch your slim self walking, running, dancing, jumping, soaring. Feel the exhilaration of your supple, responsive, healthy body. Explore and know this slender, well-knit body and enjoy its firm, cleancut lines.

Let it step out of the mirror and merge with your observing self, until there is only this one, slim you. And now, before terminating your trance state by the usual one-to-three count, choose one particular pose or movement of your new body which you like best. This will be your symbol for the new way of seeing yourself. It will not only quickly guide you back to this altered state of consciousness whenever you wish; it will also be with you in your waking state at odd intervals during the day. And as you visualize the slim graceful you more and more frequently in both the trance and waking states, you will find that reality will begin to conform to it. You will in reality think, move, and act as the slim you; and eventually this mode of thinking will permeate you so completely that your physical image will be changed by it, not only in your own mind, but in the minds of others as well.

Through the Corporeal

Since mental processes will become clear only to one who has grasped the corporeal with full clarity, any endeavour in grasping the mental processes should be made only through grasping the corporeal, not otherwise.

Nyanaponika Thera

A Point of Passage

The organism is never located in a single instant. In its life the three modes of time—the past, the present and the future—form a whole which cannot be split up into individual elements . . . We cannot describe the momentary state of an organism without taking its history into consideration and without referring it to a future state for which this state is merely a point of passage.

Ernst Cassirer

10.
Mind Room

INTRODUCTORY NOTE

A mind room is a place of many functions, a safety zone to which you can retreat to catch your breath, to restore your spirit, or to gear yourself for action. It is a place in which your mind, in its altered state of consciousness, can deal with a problem that might seem insurmountable in the reality state.

Let it become a familiar place which you can find easily even under stress, and in which you feel completely at home.

PREPARATION

It is very easily reached: just sit in a comfortable chair or lie in bed, and close your eyes. (Once you know the way, you'll also be able to find it with your eyes open.) Relax every muscle in your body, from the top of your head to the tips of your toes, and count slowly from ten to zero. Tell yourself that, on reaching zero, you will be in a very deep state of relaxation, on the threshold of your altered state of consciousness.

You may feel a tingling in your fingers and a fluttering in your eyelids. You are now passing through the door into the state of heightened awareness, in which you can tap the dormant powers of your mind.

Now the fluttering of the transition has passed, as you penetrate deeper and deeper into the recesses of your mind.

GOAL
To create a sanctuary in one's own mind.

TIME
Half an hour or more.

THE EXERCISE

You are in a very pleasant, deeply relaxed state now, basking in a drowsy sense of semi-reality, even though you are perfectly aware of the world around you—the muted noise from next door, or perhaps the sound of silence emanating from a snow-covered or sun-baked street, and the ticking of your clock. You know that you can return to this world at any moment you wish by simply opening your eyes.

But you don't wish to return just yet. You continue to allow the half-formed thoughts and images to drift around in your head, until you come to a small, cozy, comfortable room where

I Sit Content

I exist as I am, that is enough, If no other in the world be aware I sit content, And if each and all be aware I sit content.

One world is aware and by far the largest to me, and that is myself, And whether I come to my own to-day or in ten thousand or ten million years, I can cheerfully take it now, or with equal cheerfulness I can wait.

My foothold is tenon'd and mortis'd in granite, I laugh at what you call dissolution, And I know the amplitude of time.

Walt Whitman
Song of Myself

The Secrets of Great Men

This art of resting the mind and the power of dismissing from it all care and worry is probably one of the secrets of energy in our great men.

Captain J. A. Hadfield

you feel completely safe and secure. This room is your safety zone, your retreat. Whenever you enter this room, you will at once feel secure and content; all fears and apprehensions are securely locked outside, once you have entered this island of safety and closed the door. The very creak of the hinges heralds this, the click of the lock which you bolt against intrusion confirms it. Any problem that seemed overwhelming before will be easily solved here.

The room is small and intimate, furnished exactly to your taste. It contains your favorite armchair— its deeply upholstered shape supportive, its sturdy bulk protective. The floor is softly carpeted, so that you can walk or pace in relaxed comfort.

The drawn drapes that cover the windows deaden the noise of the outside world and allow only a soft light to filter through. Though you are alone in your room, this calm solitude is filled with an exhilarating sense of space and freedom. Fears, cares, discomfort have no place here. Your room is the home of well-being, where you breathe in a security free from all uncertainty. Your room is the home of your real, your best self.

Here you can safely settle down and rest until you are strong enough to emerge and confront the outside world again. Here you can let your expanded mind range over any problem you have. The room will coax your mind toward a solution, gently, slowly, surely, inevitably.

All you need do to return to ordinary consciousness is to tell yourself that you will now count slowly from one to three. At the count of three you will open your eyes. As soon as you do, you will be fully awake, and completely relaxed and unafraid, capable of dealing efficiently with whatever problem confronts you.

Rising above Negatives

Once you know any "negative" system such as fear exists you can get the energy out of it by rising above it through meditation and observation.

John C. Lilly

A Hiding Place

I have a hiding place
It can be in a closet
Sometimes it is the attic,
Other times it is in the basement
But, my favorite hiding place
    is in MYSELF.

Fran De Nardo, Gr. 6

The House of Inner Composure

I am entering a solemn house. It is called "the house of inner composure or self collection." In the background are many burning candles arranged so as to form four pyramid-like points. An old man stands at the door of the house. People enter, they do not talk and often stand still in order to concentrate. The old man at the door tells me about the visitors to the house and says: "When they leave they are pure." I enter the house now, and I am able to concentrate completely.

C. G. Jung
A patient's dream

11.
Tuning Out I

PREPARATION

A fairly deep trance state is desirable, and it takes practice to self-induce it reliably. Begin the induction using whatever technique has proved most effective for you. Close your eyes and induce progressively greater relaxation, then deepen the state further by counting slowly from ten to zero.

At the zero point, test your depth by means of ideomotor activity, e.g., raising and lowering your hand and arm through suggestion as explained in earlier exercises. When you have reached and verified an effective level, you are ready to begin.

THE EXERCISE

Since your attention is already focused on one of your hands, keep it there. But now, instead of the tingling sensation, suggest to yourself that you are about to feel a slight pain in the space between your index and middle fingers. In a moment or two allow it to travel upward, along the inner sides of both fingers, up to the tips, then around and back. From there it will spread throughout both fingers, until they are completely enveloped in this slight, but quite noticeable pain.

Allow the condition to remain for a while, concentrating on the sensation as vividly as you can. Then shift your attention to the index and middle

GOAL
To enable one to turn off awareness of physical pain. (The next few exercises are all designed for the same goal.)

TIME
At the beginning, each tuning out exercise will take approximately half an hour. As you gain facility, you will require less time; but remember that this exercise should be practiced with consistent regularity until the faculty to tune out becomes almost automatic. This faculty requires an attitude of mind which must be learned and sharpened under non-crisis conditions, so that in time of crisis the faculty will not be affected. But exercise caution in using it. Remember that pain is often a warning signal, and that eliminating it does *not* imply elimination of the cause.

fingers of your other hand, and reflect on how they would feel if they were afflicted by this pain. Concentrate deeply, trying to feel how the pain would actually feel there. The longer you think about it, the more acutely you imagine it. Now it actually seems as if there were a mirror-image pain there—as if those two fingers were trying to assume some of the pain of the afflicted ones. And, in fact, the afflicted ones do seem to hurt less now, because there is, after all, only one pain, and it is now shared equally between the two pairs of fingers.

Now allow the balance to shift decidely toward the second pair: the pain there intensifies markedly, while in the fingers of the first hand it diminishes steadily until it is hardly noticeable there. And now it is gone—you no longer feel any pain at all in the fingers where the pain began. It has been completely transferred from the first hand to the second hand.

Allow this fact to sink deeply into your mind: *A painful stimulus has been transferred from one part of your body to another.*

Now remind yourself that, no matter where the pain is located, it is still the same pain that you yourself induced. It will vanish at your bidding, just as it arose at your bidding.

Now tell yourself that the pain is about to retreat, as a moving point of light, from within the center of the fingers outward to the skin, and from there down to the space between the fingers, leaving a trail of extinguished pain behind it.

Now you feel the point of pain only in that little space between the fingers, and even there it becomes less and less acute. It recedes, like a dim light, into the distance. You have to make an effort to feel it at all. And now it is completely gone, completely extinguished.

Remain still for a moment, savoring the total absence of pain. Then, before starting your wake-up count—one, two, three—tell yourself that the next time you practice this exercise both the appearance and the disappearance of the pain will proceed much more rapidly and easily.

The Feeling of Confidence

Although I am convinced that anybody can relieve pain by light digital contact, I am equally certain that the operator must display and feel complete confidence in his ability to achieve relief in order to attain success. This factor lends further support to the pure suggestion hypothesis, since the feeling of confidence in the operator is likely to be communicated to the patient.

Eric Cuddon

The Idea of Healing

I have always been a little surprised at the disrepute into which healing has fallen in orthodox church circles. This has been, I think, because of the quackery of some of the more spectacular, popular exponents of the idea of healing. Yet steadily and quietly it has been practiced through the ages by the devout. I will say in all humility that I am convinced that I have at times been privileged to share in this ministry myself since I was first healed in 1932 in India—at which time I knew nothing about it. I am quite sure that here again is something that belongs in the realm of parapsychology. I am quite sure that it is not always psychosomatic because of the number of instances where healing occurs in a person who, for one reason or another, is unable to cooperate either because of unconsciousness or infancy or distance. The patient may have no knowledge of what is going on, and yet the phenomenon of healing occurs. I picture this as the phenomenon of God's power streaming through human collaborators into the world, in directions in which He wishes it to go.

H. L. Puxley

12.
Tuning Out II

INTRODUCTORY NOTE

To perform this exercise you must wait until you are actually in pain; but for the purpose of acquainting yourself with the technique, assume that you have caught your fingers in a closing door. They are swollen and discolored; the slightest touch is exquisitely painful, and you are doubly handicapped because it is the hand you use most that is hurt.

PREPARATION

You may not yet have delved deeply enough into your altered states of consciousness to disassociate yourself from pain; but you have learned to transfer it from one part of your body to another, and it would obviously be useful to transfer this throbbing agony to the other hand, which is less indispensable in everyday activities.

THE EXERCISE

Use the same trance induction as for Exercise 1. When you have reached sufficient depth, concentrate very intensely on the pain, experiencing it as consciously as you can, first as a whole, then in segments, finger by finger.

Gradually focus your concentration on one particular finger. Feel the pain slowly flowing out of

GOAL
To eliminate awareness of pain.

TIME
Approximately half an hour.

Both Inside and Outside

It seems that absolutely everything
both inside and outside me
is happening by itself,
yet at the same time
that I myself am doing all of it,
that my separate individuality
is simply a function,
something being done
by everything which is not me,
yet at the same time
everything which is not me
is a function
of my separate individuality.

Alan Watts

90

that finger and into the same finger on your other hand, as if they were connected by a pain-conducting tube.

Be very patient, and do not try to rush this process. When you have succeeded in draining the pain out of one finger, begin on the next one, and then the next, until all pain has been shifted from one hand to the other.

End the practice session with a self-suggestion that this transferred state will continue after you wake up, and will be in effect for the remainder of that day. Then awaken yourself by the one-two-three count.

The next day, while repeating the exercise, try adding a self-suggestion to the effect that the pain will be much less intense than the day before.

NOTE

In these exercises use your judgment, and proceed at your own pace. If you overload your unconscious mind with more demands than it can handle at one time, it will not respond; this can prove discouraging. On the other hand, each positive response, no matter how slight, will reinforce the success pattern, and encourage you in subsequent exercises.

CAUTION

In cases where a pain is your body's signal that medical treatment is necessary, this exercise should not be used as a substitute for medicine or a doctor's care. The exercise is presented here to demonstrate that the mind can sometimes help relieve bodily pain, in much the same way that drugs and other chemicals do. We repeat that this exercise is in no way a substitute for first aid or for necessary professional medical help.

An Offer to Cure

Robed in my wig and gown, I was about to conduct a divorce case in London for a provincial firm of solicitors. Their managing clerk, accompanied by a colleague from the office of their London agents, met me outside the Court. The former had a splitting headache; he had taken aspirin without relief.

I offered to cure the headache, but the afflicted man scoffed; he bet me half a crown that I would be unable to do so in three minutes, as I had suggested. I sat down beside him on a bench in the corridor of the Court and started my stop watch, inviting him to let me know at once when his headache was gone. His colleague from the agents was a witness.

I laid my hands on the incapacitated clerk, and two and a half minutes later he stated he no longer had any trace of a headache. Willingly, but surprisedly, he paid the half-crown forfeit.

Eric Cuddon

13.
Tuning Out III

PREPARATION

A light state of trance will suffice to activate you, especially after the first few times. At the beginning, close your eyes while talking yourself into relaxation. Later, with practice, you will learn to relax profoundly with your eyes open, e.g., by looking fixedly at one point. At times you may need to engage in this exercise in the presence of other people, when you don't wish to attract attention to yourself.

Count silently from ten down to zero, reminding yourself that at the count of zero your altered state of consciousness will be fully established.

THE EXERCISE

See yourself in your dentist's chair, feel his instrument gently probing your teeth; smell the scent of soap and antiseptic that permeates the room.

Now the probe has found a tender spot and you wince, less in pain than in apprehension of worse to come. You watch tensely while he prepares to fill the cavity, and inserts an attachment into the drill.

Now he rests it against the tender spot, pushes the foot pedal; the drill begins to buzz and vibrate and you grip the arms of the chair. You feel the too-familiar crescendo of pain as the drill

GOAL
To eliminate physical pain, by experiencing the effect of an analgesic without actually taking the drug.

TIME
Depending on your familiarity with the drug whose effect you are trying to duplicate, this exercise will take from fifteen minutes to half an hour. Practice it frequently while you are not in pain, so that the pathway will be well established when you need it.

92

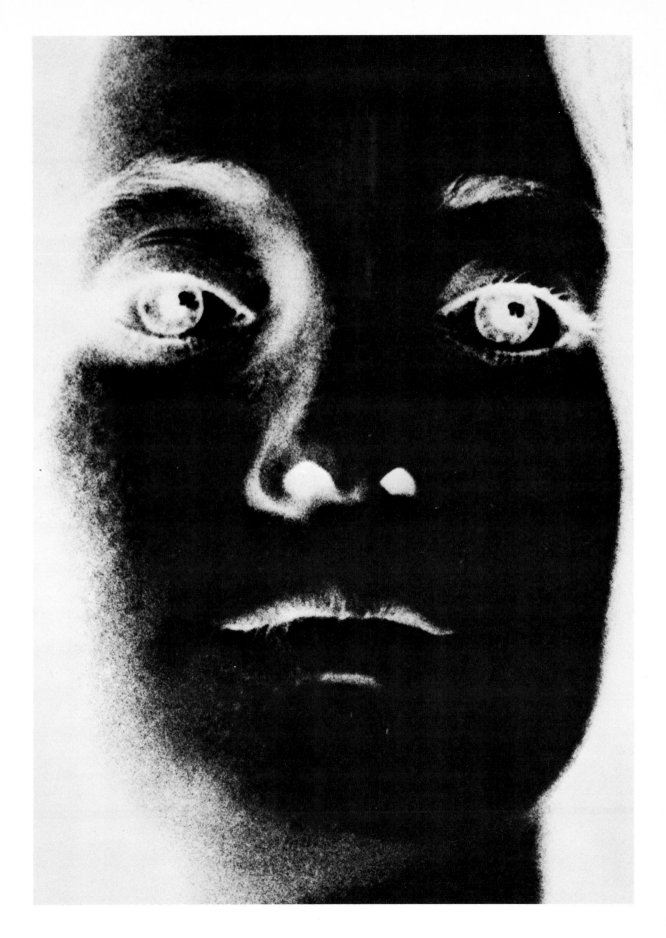

advances toward the nerve, and realize that you will need novocaine to endure what is to follow.

The novocaine needle penetrates your gum. There is an instant of pain—then the contents of the syringe take over, already dulling sensation at the point of impact.

Now you relax while the numbness spreads, along your lips and along your tongue. There is nothing more to worry about. The drilling starts again, and you know that it must be very close to the nerve now; but, blissfully, you feel nothing at all, except the almost disembodied touch of the instrument. You bask in this total absence of all sensation. In your mind you follow every step of the procedure, aware of everything the dentist does, but aware also that nothing can touch you, that all pain is kept at bay behind an impenetrable barrier.

Then the job is finished, and you see yourself getting out of the chair, smiling with some difficulty because of your numb lips.

Concentrate on this feeling for a few more moments. Then begin your wake-up count, telling yourself that the numbness will begin to diminish now that the effect of the novocaine wears off, and will have vanished entirely by the time you open your eyes.

You can vary this exercise by using different pain sites and different drugs. After a few practice sessions, test your mettle against your next real headache: reach for your mind instead of for the aspirin.

All Shall Be Well

There is the question of the very meaning of the assertion "All shall be well, and all shall be well, and all manner of thing shall be well." I can say only that the meaning of the assertion is the experience itself. Outside that state of consciousness it has no meaning, so much so that it would be difficult even to believe in it as a revelation without the actual experience. For the experience makes it perfectly clear that the whole universe is through and through the playing of love in every shade of the word's use, from animal lust to divine charity. Somehow this includes even the holocaust of the biological world, where every creature lives by feeding on others. Our usual picture of this world is reversed so that every victim is seen as offering itself in sacrifice.

Alan Watts

A Man from Maine

Phineas Quimby was probably the most famous mesmerist (hypnotist) in mid-nineteenth century America. A clockmaker by trade, this man from Maine had about six weeks of formal schooling in his life. The mesmeric art fascinated him, and as he practiced it he gradually drew away from clockmaking, set up an office to treat patients for a wide variety of ailments, and received the title of "Doctor" from apparently grateful patients who came to him from all over New England. The most famous of his patients was the future Mary Baker Eddy, who visited him at his Portland office after twenty-four years of invalidism, was treated by him, and returned to her home apparently cured. The beginnings of Christian Science, according to many historians, date from that visit.

Allan Angoff

14.

Listen to the Hands

GOAL
To control or eliminate physical pain.

TIME
Approximately ten minutes at each practice session.

PREPARATION

You require an altered state of consciousness to learn this exercise; but once you have mastered it, it will work instantly in whatever state of consciousness you find yourself when you need it.

Sit in a straight-backed chair, with both hands on your lap, palms up. Induce a trance state by closing your eyes and silently verbalizing suggestions of relaxation. Follow up with a slow count from ten to zero, suggesting that your trance will have deepened by the time you reach zero.

THE EXERCISE

If you do not by now feel the trance-threshold-tingling in one or both of your hands, tell yourself that you will now count from one to three. On reaching three you will feel, in your weaker hand, some sensation that is different from the normal. Do not suggest what it will be like—wait for it to manifest itself.

It may take one of many forms: your hand may feel asleep, or as if it were encased in a glove; it may tingle or vibrate; it may seem to be made of wood; it may feel cold, or it may seem to have become a thing altogether apart from you. What-

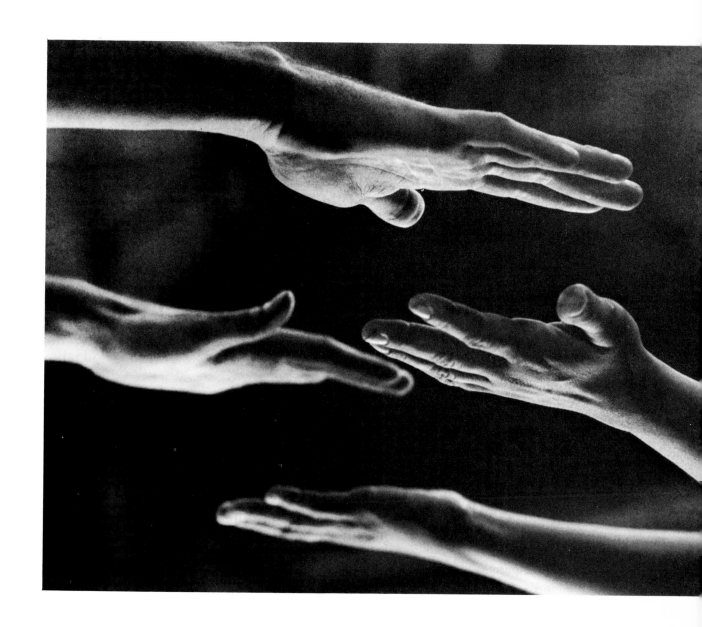

15.

Black Light

PREPARATION

Find a location as free as possible from noise and distraction. Lower shades, close blinds, turn off lights; if necessary, wear an eye mask and use earplugs. It helps if you are physically tired rather than energetic, and your stomach is empty rather than full.

Roll your eyeballs upward and focus on a point uncomfortably high above your line of vision; keep them in that position while closing your eyes, and for some moments thereafter. You will find that this helps you to enter your trance state. Now, deepen the trance by relaxing all your muscles, not forcing it but nurturing and monitoring your gradual descent.

THE EXERCISE

As you go deeper and deeper, the room seems to descend with you, going further and further down with you until it is an underground prison cell in which you are locked. There is no light, and the silence is so profound that you feel you are alone in a pit of emptiness, totally deserted in tomblike stillness.

GOAL
To deal with difficult or unbearable stress situations.

TIME
This exercise will be most effective if you can provide for a fairly long undisturbed period (approximately one hour). You may not need the entire hour to do the exercise, but you need to know that a full hour is available if you want and need it.

Enter into this total silence with all your senses. You reach out with your hand and feel the clammy texture of a wall which no sunlight has ever touched. Your eyes try to discern an outline in the blackness, but to no avail. Your ears strain for the slightest sound of life, but there is none; even the sound of your breathing is lost in the stillness.

A Stimulus-free Environment

Keen: What happens to your body when you are in a stimulus-free environment?

Lilly: You can forget your body and concentrate on the workings of your mind. But if any stimulus remains it becomes overwhelming. Once when I was in the tank a series of bubbles formed from the water and began to hit my foot. As each bubble traveled up my leg I experienced an exquisite pleasure. In fact, the pleasure was so great that it turned to pain when the bubbles began to come at about five-second intervals.

A Conversation with John Lilly

A Relief

Crying
is a relief

for those
remaining alive
a new re/lease
on life.

I remember
when my body knew
when it was time
to cry
and it was all
right then

to explode
the world
and melt
everything
warm

and start new
washed clean.

Bernard Gunther

Through the Problem

Release in extremity
lies through
and not away from
the problem.

Alan Watts

You feel yourself becoming a part of this unearthly silence, so that even you can no longer make a sound to break it.

You feel you cannot stand this for another minute, yet you know that you must—for days, weeks, months. You begin to sense the demands that will be made upon your sanity at the very thought of your situation. You are imprisoned in this unbearably endless void, and you must somehow survive here.

At this point, focus your attention on your body and slowly, consciously, relax every inch of it, from the top of your head to the very tips of your toes. Tell yourself that you will count from ten to zero, as you have done so often before; and that, when you have reached zero, your mind will present to you the recollection of one of the happiest days of your life. There is no need to strain your mind or search for images. Simply count to zero, stay relaxed, and let the pleasant recollection arise in your mind gradually and easily. Let the picture be like a landscape seen hazily at a distance, becoming clearer and clearer as you approach.

Now the happy picture fills your whole mind, and it is so incredibly vivid and detailed that it is no longer a recollection but a re-living. You are truly there, in the time and place of this happy memory; you relive it exactly as it happened, through all your senses—what you saw, what you heard, everything you touched, or smelled, or tasted. You are fully re-living the original experience.

The darkness and terror of the soundproof cell have disappeared as if they had never existed, just like the reality in which you are performing this exercise: For the moment, and for as long as you choose, nothing exists except the reality of this re-lived happiness. You know that you will be able to summon this happy experience again whenever you wish. And you also know that you will, as always, return from this place by telling yourself that, after counting from one to three and opening your eyes, you will be back in your state of everyday consciousness, feeling perfectly relaxed and at ease, capable of dealing with whatever stresses come your way.

The Basic Text

Memory is the basic text for the self-teacher. The creative person exploits and exhausts every possibility of the mind, conscious and unconscious. He celebrates experience and his own creative ability in the face of death. I have observed this increased awareness of the basic elements—the sensations of life—come alive in older persons of all talents, colors, shapes and textures as they become free of the encumbrances of daily routine.

Robert N. Butler

A True Life of the Imagination

The long hours I spent piecing together my future revenge were so intense that I began to feel as if the project were already under way. Every night, and even parts of the day, I wandered through Paris as if my escape were already a fact. As I write these thoughts I had so many years ago, thoughts that come back now to assail me with such terrible clarity, I am struck by how absolute silence and total isolation were able to lead a young man shut up in a cell into a true life of the imagination.

Henri Charrière
Papillon

And There Was Lots of Light

I kept looking—and it was all black—I kept looking and trying to find what I was looking for—and when I did find it, my whole spine was just going up and down—I was shivering up and down and there was lots of light.

Paul Bindrim
From a Sharing Session

It Suffices Only to Wish

We do not understand that life is paradise, for it suffices only to wish to understand it, and at once paradise will appear in front of us in its beauty.

Feyodor Dostoevski
The Brothers Karamazov

16.

Talisman

INTRODUCTORY NOTE

The mind in an altered state of consciousness has its own talismans, and uses them much as it uses them in the usual reality state. But because the unconscious layers of the mind which are tapped in altered states are very responsive to symbols, their effect is greatly enhanced.

PREPARATION

Settle down comfortably on a sofa, bed, or in an armchair. Roll your eyes upward and fix them on a point much higher than your line of vision. When they tire, let them close, keeping your eyes focused on that high point while your lids close over them.

Now tell yourself that, in order to go deeper and deeper into your altered state of consciousness, you will count from ten to zero; and that, on reaching zero, you will be at a much deeper level of mind than now. Feel yourself descending to that deeper level while visualizing the downward progression of numerals: 10, 9, 8, 7, 6, 5, 4, 3, 2, 1, 0. Deeper and deeper—very deeply now.

GOAL
To improve memory and concentration in a wide variety of areas, by the use of symbols and post-trance self-suggestion.

TIME
Approximately 15 minutes.

THE EXERCISE

Now that you have reached a fairly deep level of altered consciousness, evoke before your mind a problem or circumstance whose solution requires better memory or improved faculties of concentration. Perhaps you have trouble with one of your courses in school. If so, say the name of the subject to yourself, and visualize the surroundings in which the course is given. See the room, the teacher, your fellow students, and yourself

Waiting for Some Power

Men have never fully used
the powers they possess
to advance the good in life,
because they have waited upon
some power external to themselves
and to nature
to do the work
they are responsible for doing.

John Dewey

among them. Now let this picture dissolve, and replace it with an image of the place where you normally do your studying for this course—your room at home, your desk, and yourself sitting before it, with textbook open before you. And while you are there, lightly place together the thumb and forefinger of either hand.

Tell yourself that, from now on, you will tremendously increase your understanding of the lectures and your subsequent recall of the material covered by simply placing your thumb and index finger in this position while you listen. The same will apply to your own studying, if you let your thumb and index finger touch lightly while reading your assignment. The touching thumb and index finger form a closed circle, and this magic circle will prevent any of the information from escaping you.

Tell yourself also that, if at any time in the future you have difficulty in recalling a specific item of information in this course, you will be able to recall it immediately by lightly closing your thumb and index finger of either hand. The magic circle will always work its magic.

Let yourself dwell on this thought for a few moments, while picturing yourself employing the magic-circle technique, effortlessly absorbing and retaining the material of your school course.

Then tell yourself that you will now count from one to three and open your eyes. As soon as you have opened them you will be back in your usual reality state, feeling very relaxed and at the same time very alert.

Repeat this exercise frequently in your altered state of consciousness until the positive reaction becomes habitual. In between, employ the technique in your ordinary waking state for recalling specific details, in order to strengthen the pattern.

This technique can be used not only for the recall and absorption of facts in school or at work, but also for more esoteric purposes, such as recapturing a mood, or reactivating a sense of motivation in any area.

I Used to Understand

O what have I forgotten since I took
Lessons in logic from a borrowed
   book?
What was it that I used to understand
But have let slip between my heart
   and hand?

Edward Davison

RELATING

17.
Intimacy

Achieving and maintaining close personal relationships is an art for which some lucky individuals have a native genius. Many people, however, find this art harder to master than any other. The impulse to relate is often blocked by shyness, pride, or fear of rejection. Resisting the need to relate creates a vicious cycle, because the longer the need is suppressed, the more the ability to relate atrophies. One way to begin revitalizing it is to "practice" a sense of intimacy with inanimate objects.

AN EXAMPLE

Such an interaction is described in Jan de Hartog's novel *The Captain*, the story of a Dutch tugboat captain and his ship. World War II has catapulted the inexperienced young tugboat master into the position of Commodore of the Dutch tugboat fleet. Used to the lonely life of a relief captain without a ship to call his own, he has developed a protective layer of detachment. Now, suddenly, he finds himself permanent master of the flag ship *Isabel Kwel*. After the baptism of fire of their first enemy engagement he awakens to a new and precious reality—the close personal tie between the captain and his ship:

I . . . had finally entered into that most ancient, mystical relationship between man and matter: the comradeship between a sailor and his ship. I was at last . . . imbuing a

GOAL
To develop the ability to form meaningful relationships.

TIME
Allow 30 minutes.

110

piece of man-made machinery with a personality of its own, linked to it by a bond of loyalty and devotion, an umbilical cord of love . . . Innocently, I put my hand on the wall beside my bunk, for the first time knowingly touching my ship in a gesture of intimacy. I looked at that wall, then at the ceiling, the door, the portholes while, within me, a new and unknown tenderness hesitantly reached out toward them, the intimate details of the sensuous body of the *Isabel Kwel* . . . I reveled in that new and unknown sense of security which the very touch of her gave me.

PREPARATION

Make yourself comfortable and close your eyes. Visualize a calm sea under a sunny, blue sky, and yourself on a ship, almost suspended in the expanse of sky and water.

See yourself looking over the railing of this ship—your ship—and follow the movement of the waves from crest to trough, one following the other in unbroken succession, while you relax muscle after muscle in a similar fluid movement.

Now single out one particular wave to follow behind your closed lids. Tell yourself that when you have traced its path through ten successions of crest and trough you will be in a very deep state of altered consciousness, much deeper than you are now.

THE EXERCISE

Now put yourself into the young captain's place. The ship you are standing on is your very own ship. Feel the smooth grain of the wooden railing under your hand, the planks of the deck under your feet as you walk toward your cabin.

Open the door—feel the door knob—enter the cabin, and lie down on the bunk. Touch the wall alongside the bunk, and compare the grainy tex-

Here Alive Together

The alienation of Western man is partly due to his having lost contact with all natural functions: the reality of being alive. There are no ends in life, only processes. Change. Spiritual reality is physical reality, clearly seen. We are all here alive together in this world at this time so what are we going to do?

Bill Voyd

A Conscious Tool

To get high is to forget yourself.
And to forget yourself
is to see everything else.
And to see everything else
is to become an understanding
molecule in evolution,
a conscious tool
of the universe.

Jerry Garcia

The Craftsman and his Tools

Labor is not merely an expenditure of energy but the personalized work of a man whose activities are sensuously directed toward preparing, fashioning, and finally decorating his product for human use. The craftsman guides the tool, not the tool the craftsman. Any alienation that may exist between the craftsman and his product is immediately overcome, as Friedrich Wilhelmsen emphasized, "by an artist judgment—a judgment bearing on a thing to be made". The tool amplifies the powers of the craftsman as a man as a human; it amplifies his power to impart his artistry, his very identity as a creative being, on raw materials.

Murray Bookchin

In Every Particular

I have always felt a life and a bliss in everything—I mean in every particular, in stones and chairs and mantelpieces and paper as well as in what is ordinarily called life: and it is through my meeting with these particulars, living and what are usually thought of as other than living, that I establish communion, feel myself mingled, with the bliss beyond.

Victor Gollancz

ture of the wall with the smooth texture of the railing. Listen to the comforting rhythm of the creaks of this bulky, seaworthy, trustworthy ship . . . and feel, as intensely as you can, the emotions which the ship aroused in the young captain.

When you have experienced these sensations as vividly as you can, tell yourself that you will now count from one to five. On reaching five, you will have fully assumed your own identity again, while still remaining in your deeply altered state of consciousness.

Leave the captain's ship now, and structure a background more in keeping with your own life situation. Take your new ability to relate to inanimate objects with you, and introduce it into the new environment. Enhance it by as many details as your imagination can conjure up, gradually adding plants, flowers, and an imaginary pet to the inanimate objects.

When you are ready to conclude the exercise, tell yourself that you will now count slowly from one to three and open your eyes. As soon as you open them, you will be back in your usual reality state, feeling very relaxed and at ease, knowing that you have taken a long step on the road toward intimacy, and that this road will become easier and easier to find every time you practice the art of intimacy.

18.

Growing Down

Because it has been some time since you were Alice's age, it is better to make the journey backward in two stages: First to Alice's actual age and appearance; then, during the second exercise, farther down into the core of her imagination, into the smaller and smaller girl she becomes by magic.

PREPARATION

Sit in a comfortable armchair with a back high enough for you to rest your head on, or lie down. Close your eyes and relax your body as completely as you can, from the top of your head to the very tips of your toes. Let yourself sink deeper and deeper into this state of relaxation, mentally and physically—deeper, deeper, deeper. Now tell yourself that you will count slowly from ten down to zero. As you do this, visualize the numbers in a downward progression, as if each successive number were standing one step lower on a staircase. Tell yourself that when you have reached zero you will be in a very deeply altered state of consciousness, much deeper than you are now. Feel the relaxation spreading throughout every muscle and nerve of your body as you count.

GOAL
Time regression to childhood, preparatory to entering into the adventures of Alice in Wonderland.

TIME
30-40 minutes.

114

THE EXERCISE

Tell yourself that you will again count from ten to zero, and that now each number will represent a year's step backward in time, so that, when you reach zero, you will be ten years younger than you are now. In your mind's eye, see the numerals of your new age.

Now pause for a few moments to recapture this ten-years-younger you. Explore this 'you' with your trance-sharpened memory rather than with your imagination. See yourself as you were then. See the face that looked at you in the mirror—your hair, your skin. Feel your body ten years ago, younger, more supple. Enter into the thoughts and feelings you experienced at that time.

A Long Time

It takes one a long time to become young.

Pablo Picasso

Our Past Years

**O joy! that in our embers
Is something that doth live,
That nature yet remembers
What was so fugitive!
The thought of our past years in me
    doth breed
Perpetual benediction.**

William Wordsworth

When you have steeped yourself so thoroughly in this recollection that it is no longer remembrance but actuality, tell yourself that you will once again count backwards, beginning with the number of your age minus ten. Visualize that number. Now, each number will represent an additional year taken off your new (trance) age, your age ten years ago. Then count backward, slowly, beginning ten years ago, and visualize clearly each number until you get to six—Alice's age in *Alice in Wonderland*.

Now you are Alice's age. More than that—you *are* Alice. You are her size; you think as she thinks; you speak as she speaks; her curiosity, her imagination are yours.

Pause and allow your mind to be saturated with these Alice thoughts. Then tell yourself that you will presently return to your customary state of consciousness by counting from one to three and opening your eyes. But first, there is one more thing you will have to do:

Tell yourself that when you are ready to embark upon the next "Alice" exercise, you will compress this journey back to her age into an instant. Once you have reached your desired trance depth you need merely say to yourself "Alice," and you will at once *be* Alice, as vividly and as completely as you are now.

Now count from one to three, and open your eyes. You are now completely back in your everyday state of reality, feeling very relaxed, very comfortable, and in excellent health.

The Swing

How do you like to go up in a swing,
Up in the air so blue?
Oh, I do think it the pleasantest thing
Ever a child can do!

Up in the air and over the wall,
Till I can see so wide,
Rivers and trees and cattle and all
Over the countryside—

Till I look down on the garden green,
Down on the roof so brown—
Up in the air I go flying again,
Up in the air and down!

Robert Louis Stevenson

19.
Ten Inches Old

GOAL
Time regression to Alice's age; body image change to the ten-inch size she becomes during one of her adventures.

TIME
30-45 minutes.

PREPARATION

Let your eyes close easily and let your entire body relax, from the top of your head to the very tips of your toes, as you go deeper and deeper into your altered state of consciousness. Deeper and deeper . . . very deeply now. Count slowly from ten to zero, and tell yourself that when you have reached zero, you will be as deeply relaxed, and as deeply in trance, as you were during the first Alice exercise.

(Pause for the count from ten to zero)
Now that you are in that same deep trance state, remember the key word you chose during the earlier exercise—the word "Alice." Whenever you are ready, say the word "Alice" to yourself, and at the same time picture the letters of the word in your mind's eye. As soon as you have done this, you will *be* Alice again, as vividly and completely as you were during the first exercise.

Thoughts in a Summer Garden

What wondrous life in this I lead!
Ripe apples drop upon my head;
The luscious clusters of the vine
Upon my mouth do crush their wine;

The nectarine and curious peach
Into my hands themselves do reach;
Stumbling on melons, as I pass,
Ensnared with flowers, I fall on grass.

Andrew Marvell

At the Edge of a Forest

What is, for example, the attitude of different people toward a forest? A painter who has gone there to paint, the owner of the forest who wishes to evaluate his business prospects, an officer who is interested in the tactical problem of defending the area, a hiker who wants to enjoy himself— each of them will have an entirely different concept of the forest because a different aspect is significant to each one. The painter's experience will be one of form and color; the businessman's of size, number, and age of the trees; the officer's of visibility and protection; the hiker's of trails and motion. While they can all agree to the abstract statement that they stand at the edge of a forest, the different kinds of activity they are set to accomplish will determine their experience of "seeing a forest."

Erich Fromm

The Giving and the Receiving

Go to your fields and your gardens, and you shall learn that it is the pleasure of the bee to gather honey of the flower, But it is also the pleasure of the flower to yield its honey to the bee. For to the bee a flower is a fountain of life, And to the flower a bee is a messenger of love, And to both, bee and flower, the giving and the receiving of pleasure, is a need and an ecstasy.

Kahlil Gibran
The Prophet

THE EXERCISE

Now that you are Alice, you would like to share some of her adventures. Alice sees that lovely garden behind the small door, at the end of the small passage, and you decide to walk in that lovely garden. But at your present size you cannot squeeze through the narrow opening and, like Alice, you decide that you must shrink like a telescope. But you do not need to drink the contents of the bottle which Alice discovered so conveniently; all you need is your mind. Tell yourself that you will once again count from ten to zero, and with each number you will grow a little smaller. When you have reached zero you will be small enough to get through the little door and the passage into the lovely garden. Like Alice, you will be ten inches tall.

(Pause for the count from ten to zero)
Now you are tiny enough to walk down the little passage into the lovely garden. Flowers of every hue are in bloom and create a kaleidoscope of colors. The grass is green and springy beneath your feet. The air is filled with the murmur of bees and cool water splashes in the fountains. The sun is warm on your cheek and the fragrant scents of summer fill your nostrils. Give yourself completely to the experience and open all your senses to this beauty.

There is too much to absorb in one visit. You will come here again, often. But now it is time to grow again to Alice's real size and then to your own real size. Tell yourself that you will count from one to three, twice. After you have reached three on the first count you will be Alice's original size. At the end of the second count you will be your own original size. You will also be back in your everyday state of consciousness, feeling relaxed, happy and immeasurably enriched by your experience.

Spring

I know where the windflowers blow! I know. I have been where the little rabbits run, I and warm yellow sun!

Diane Jurkovic, Grade 2
P.S. 148, Queens

Something Like a Glimmering

Your poetry issues of its own accord when you and the object have become one — When you have plunged deep enough into the object to see something like a hidden glimmering there.

Basho

In the Human Eye

Man is incomprehensible without Nature, and Nature is incomprehensible apart from man. For the delicate loveliness of the flower is as much in the human eye as in its own fragile petals, and the splendor of the heavens as much in the imagination that kindles at the touch of their glory as in the shining of countless worlds.

Hamilton Wright Mabie

121

20.

Penelope's Cave

PREPARATION

Close your eyes and enter your altered state of consciousness by means of relaxation suggestions. As you go deeper and deeper, see yourself on a hot summer day in the country. In the distance you see the figure of a young girl—Penelope.

THE EXERCISE

Visualize Penelope as clearly as you can, getting in close to her, focusing on her face. Picture yourself tracing her features with the fingers of your right hand, passing them lightly over her forehead, eyes, nose, and lips. Now lift your hand to your own face, and feel the shape of her forehead on yours, the shape of her eyes, her nose, and her lips. See how alike they feel; they could belong to the same face; they *are* the same face —your face; you are going to live her life for a while.

You are sitting on a riverbank now. Feel the stillness of the hot summer afternoon as you sit there. It is so quiet—so still that everything in you is hushed in response. Close your eyes to savor this peace, this silence. It is quite hot, but you know that there is also shade and coolness here, the coolness of a nearby cave.

GOAL
To teach one to experience adventures that happened to someone else —either a real person or an imaginary one. In this exercise the someone else is a young girl, Penelope, who goes to explore a cave.

TIME
At least fifteen to twenty minutes should be allowed for this exercise. Those who wish may linger in the cave for a longer time.

As you think about the cave, it seems to come toward you, behind your closed lids; and the closer it comes, the more inviting it is . . . Now it stops in front of you, inviting you to enter.

How cool it is inside. A narrow path leads into the depth of the mountain. It meanders downhill, very gently, very gradually becoming a little steeper as you become accustomed to the dim light, to the coolness, the peacefulness. Now the path is becoming smoother and smoother, and walking requires less and less effort. And you know that soon, very soon now, it will cease being a path altogether; you will not have to walk at all any more, but will be able to float down comfortably, enjoyably, effortlessly, down to the depths of the cave waiting to receive you.

Now you feel yourself beginning to float, hardly aware of the transition from walking. It is a warm, secure, happy feeling to descend like this, cradled on a soft pillow of air, watching the scenery go by as you float deeper and deeper.

And now that the burden of walking has been lifted from you, you have time to see the walls of this cave. As you look around this tunnel through which you are floating, the walls are lined with pictures. The scenes are very familiar, and gradually you realize that they depict scenes from your childhood, recalling your happiest memories. And as you continue to float down, the pictures of your happy memories accompany you down the corridor of time, back through the years of your childhood, year by year. Whenever you wish, you may slow down to examine a picture at leisure, and continue to float when you are ready.

Now you have found a picture at which you want to stop. You have stopped now, and are examining it, seeing it in all its vividness of color, all its detail. And as you absorb these colors and these details, you also absorb the feeling of happiness you experienced when you first encountered that scene as a child. The happiness penetrates you, until it encompasses and fills your whole mind. And you know that this feeling of happiness, of well-being, will remain with you,

No Need for Words

It was a morning in early summer. A silver haze shimmered and trembled over the lime trees. The air was laden with their fragrance. The temperature was like a caress. I remember—I need not recall—that I climbed up a tree stump and felt suddenly immersed in Itness. I did not call it by that name. I had no need for words. It and I were one.

Bernard Berenson

The Commonest Things

The commonest things of nature have qualities and characteristics which are stupendous. They are a revelation to the persons who study and analyze them. Most people, however, find only strange and unusual things worth wondering about, while they take ordinary things for granted.

Saint Augustine

Extend Your Horizon

Through entering into a series of experiences designed to revitalize your sense of smell, touch, and taste, you can extend your horizon of awareness. Participation in experiences designed to foster what has been called sensory Awakening can enhance your capacity for selective awareness—so that you can open yourself to awareness either at will or spontaneously.

Herbert A. Otto

even as you float back up, slowly, effortlessly, past the earlier pictures, all the way back up to the path. Now you retrace that path, leading smoothly upward, outward, toward the sunlight which you begin to see in the distance. Now the light comes closer, grows brighter, and you begin to feel the warmth and the stillness of the summer day again. You come closer and closer to the mouth of the cave, and now you are outside once again, out in the daylight again, but with the happiness of your past memories alive within you. Without losing any of the happiness, any of the memories, separate yourself mentally from Penelope, and leave her sitting on the riverbank. Tell yourself that you will now count from one to three, and then quietly open your eyes in the present again.

Language of the World Inside

Symbolic language is language in which we express inner experience as if it were a sensory experience, as if it were something we were doing or something that was done to us in the world of things. Symbolic language is language in which the world outside is a symbol of the world inside, a symbol for our souls and our minds.

Erich Fromm

21.
Offstage

To allow yourself to express genuine feelings and emotions, and to enhance your ability to communicate meaningfully with others.

TIME
Before doing this exercise within a structured time frame, you may have to put in time on two other specific exercises: (1) to construct a refuge location (real or imaginary) in your mind; (2) to establish an interpersonal relationship in your mind, with someone (real or imaginary) to whom you feel you can talk freely and naturally.

INTRODUCTORY NOTE

If you have performed the Mind Room exercise in Section I, you have already built your refuge; if not, look for the right place now. Let your mind roam freely. The refuge may be a house or a room, it may be indoors, outdoors, spacious, small, majestic, cozy, elegant, homey, or anything else you want it to be. But once you have chosen your place of refuge, stick with it, and furnish it with great attention to detail. In the future, these details will be your landmarks. They will always show you the way to your refuge quickly and easily.

PREPARATION

An imaginary person is sometimes harder to create than an imaginary place. You may already know someone wise enough to be a trusted advisor—a teacher, a grandparent, a community leader. But this person is likely to be older than you—too old, really, to serve as a close friend, to understand the feelings of someone your age. Yet, with a little trance-alteration, that person may well turn out to be the perfect choice for the present purpose.

Put yourself into an altered state of consciousness by counting from ten to zero and relaxing muscle after muscle.

THE EXERCISE

When you have reached your deeper level of consciousness let the image of the person you have imagined fill your mind. The eyes are sympathetic, intent. The poise of the head expresses readiness to listen and to respond. Now, while keeping your trance at a steady depth, allow this image to recede slowly, very slowly, as if it were going down the length of a tunnel.

This is the tunnel of time. As the image recedes into the tunnel, it travels backward in time, one year, two years, five years, ten years . . . until the person has reached the age you want him or her to be. Your friend's appearance has not really changed; the face is still the familiar one you know so well. Only the generation gap has been eliminated. You can talk freely, confident that you will be understood on your own terms.

Now, together, go to your mental place of refuge. Settle down in your haven of security and peace. Feel the current of silent communication flowing between you. Now let that current express itself in words that travel from one open heart to another. There is no fear of being misunderstood, of getting enmeshed in man-made static. Your every word is carried along on this strong current of communication. You are at one with the person to whom you are speaking. Your moods, thoughts, and words are shared. The moments of silence are filled with a relaxed oneness.

Reaching Out Toward the Other

The overtones are lost,
and what is left are conversations
which, in their poverty, cannot hide
the lack of real contact.
We glide past each other.
But why? Why—?

We reach out towards the other. In vain—because we have never dared to give ourselves.

Dag Hammarskjöld

To Feel More Connected

There is an increasing concern for the humanization of organizations, an increasing desire by people to feel more connected with each other, to act on their own environment rather than feeling acted upon.

Vladimir Dupre

Still a Long Way to Go

When he told me that he had many friends, could easily make new ones and have a high old time with them, it struck hard like a blow which had been very carefully aimed. A question had become meaningless.

I only understood much later, understood that his words had hurt so because my love had still a long way to go before it would mature into—love. Understood that he had reacted instinctively and justifiably in self-defense, and with a sure sense of what was the right path for me and for him.

Dag Hammarskjöld

It is pure joy to understand and to be understood, to know that every inflection of your voice is heard, every nuance of your mood perceived. You know, too, that you are being yourself at last, that you have surrendered your mask. It is as if through this communication a new, more genuine, more real you had come to life.

At the end of the exercise, just before awakening yourself by counting from one to three and opening your eyes, tell yourself that next time you will find your secret place very easily, that your words in conversation will flow very smoothly and confidently; and that you will, today and always, emerge from this experience with a feeling of great serenity, peace and self-confidence, more capable than ever before of dealing with problems of communication and of relating to others —in all states of consciousness.

22.
Joy

INTRODUCTORY NOTE

This exercise is designed to be performed by a group of people (not more than six or eight) sitting in a circle. Place a glass of water in front of each group member, and a large, empty pitcher in the center of the circle.

PREPARATION

The altered state of consciousness may be induced by softly cadenced repetitive phrases, evocative of relaxation. They may be spoken by one member of the group, called the reader, or by the group as a whole. If, by now, you have acquired a favorite private trance-induction ritual, you may find it very effective to superimpose it silently on the words spoken aloud. Such a double-barreled approach often enhances the trance effect.

THE EXERCISE

Now you are completely relaxed, from the top of your head to the tips of your toes. Your eyes are open, and you are mentally alert, yet completely relaxed, as you think about the water in the glass before you. You realize that it represents joy—a

GOAL
To develop a sense of interpersonal unity and to eliminate feelings of alienation through the sharing of joy, in a joint symbolic venture.

TIME
The timing of this exercise is necessarily dependent on the participants' availability, which is most likely to be late afternoon or evening. This is, coincidentally, a good time of day for a shared symbolic experience.

joy that is yours, a joy that no one can take from you, a joy that may have been private—or even forgotten—till now, perhaps going far back to your childhood; or it may be a joy of more recent origin. You know best which it is, because you are in complete command of yourself, in this as in all other states of consciousness. Your joy is in that glass. Relive it again in all its intensity.

Now the pitcher is to be passed around the circle. It is a time for sharing joy with each other. As the pitcher is passed around, each participant pours the water from his glass into the pitcher. As you slowly pour the water from your glass into the pitcher you grasp with the very essence of your being that you are engaged in a common purpose—the sharing of joy. You are adding your share of private joy to the common pool, and thereby become truly united with every other member of your group, in a unity of sharing.

At the Heart of Pleasure

That lovely warmth moves me now as I write—my wife and the children asleep next door. It is, at bottom, the presence in me of all those I love, and it is that net of connections, that cradle of affection that seems to me at the heart of my own pleasure. Not long ago when I visited a college, a student said to me: "You seem to know just where you are; how do you do it?" I thought for a long time before answering, and I realized then for the first time that I was protected as if by a charm by the presence within me of my family and comrades. "The bird a nest, the spider a web, man friendship," writes Blake, and that is my sense of it.

Peter Marin

131

Shared Experiences

It has consistently been found that for maximum effect experiences designed to foster such sensory awakening should be shared experiences. Not only is it more fun to have these experiences in a small, congenial group, but individual growth and change appear to be more intense and lasting.

Herbert A. Otto

(In silence, allow each person as much time as he wishes to pour his glass of water into the pitcher. When the pitcher has been returned to its place in the center of the group, the reader continues.)

You realize that by pouring your joys into the pitcher you have experienced the joy of giving. But giving is only half of the joy of sharing. The other half is the joy of receiving, becoming party to the joys of every other member of the group as well.

The pitcher contains all of our individual joys blended together. Once again the pitcher will be passed around the circle, and this time each one is to fill his glass with the liquid—the shared joys of everyone here—and slowly drink it, savoring each mouthful as a multiplication of joy, as a sweetness far above the solitary enjoyment of an individual joy.

(When this has been done, the reader may continue with words such as these.)

"Some of you here may or may not have been close friends before; you may or may not become friends as a result of this experience. Whether you do or not is immaterial: the important thing is that for the duration of the exercise you have been truly one with the other members of this group and from now on you will know that, in a subtle but essential way, you are part of everyone else on earth.

"Every time you reflect on this, a wonderful feeling of belonging will suffuse you. And as you continue to reflect on it, you will find that this feeling of belonging gradually carries over into your everyday reality, enhancing and beautifying it, and supporting you in times of stress."

The exercise is ended now. Awaken yourself, individually or collectively, with a one-to-three count. After the count of three you will be back in your ordinary reality state, feeling serene, relaxed, and at ease.

The Quality of Aliveness

Similar in some ways and different in others is the symbol of water—of the ocean or of the stream. Here, too, we find the blending of change and permanence, of constant movement and yet of permanence. We also feel the quality of aliveness, continuity and energy. But there is a difference; where fire is adventurous, quick, exciting, water is quiet, slow and steady. Fire has an element of surprise; water an element of predictability. Water symbolizes the mood of aliveness, too, but one which is "heavier," "slower," and more comforting than exciting.

Erich Fromm

Love in the Right Way

If anyone, therefore, will not learn from Christianity to love himself in the right way, then neither can he love his neighbor...To love one's self in the right way and to love one's neighbor are absolutely analogous concepts, are at bottom one and the same...Hence the law is: "You shall love yourself as you love your neighbor when you love him as yourself."

Søren Kierkegaard

23.

Finding Each Other

This exercise, like the preceding one, is designed for a group of six to eight persons, sitting in a circle. A loaf of bread is required. It should be firmly textured, but soft enough to break into pieces easily, without crumbling.

GOAL
To eliminate feelings of alienation, and to develop a sense of unity with others, through the sharing of the same life source.

TIME
Like all group exercises, this one might best be planned for late afternoon or early evening. Though the exercise itself does not take long, some extra time should be allowed for reflection or meditation after it is completed.

PREPARATION

Participants should be helped to reach an altered state of consciousness through the process of relaxing the body step by step—the top of the head, the forehead, face, throat, chest, abdomen, legs, and feet. Let one member of the group, with a pleasant voice, softly speak short repetitive phrases that suggest relaxation and calm well-being.

134

THE EXERCISE

Now you are completely relaxed, your entire body, all of it. Your eyes are open and you are, at one and the same time, totally relaxed and fully alert. Look at the bread here before us, and fill your mind with all that it means, and with the images it evokes. Fields of golden wheat waving in the wind—grains of wheat pouring into bins in the flour mill—white flour in the bakery, a snow-dusting over everything; the scent of fresh-baked bread, crisp crust, softly warm inside. *(Pause.)* Bread is life, the staff of life; making bread is like creating life, the yeast in the dough making it rise and live. To break bread is the sign of friend-ship and love. Discover again the joy of bread in your hands, crunching between your teeth, satis-fying hunger.

This loaf evokes such similar and individual thoughts in all of us. It is our loaf, full of all that

The Better Thing

**It is better
to give
and receive.**

> **Bernard Gunther**

If We Listen Carefully

Around the table of death and life, bread and wine, where we can still meet each other, there are sounds to hear if we listen carefully. There is the sound of going down into the abyss and being lifted up, heart and body, not to heaven but to the good earth. There are the sounds of the lively ghosts of God, laughing still with love. There are the sounds of men and women stirring, standing. There is the sound of the season's changing. And wine. There is the sound of day breaking. And bread.

> **James Carroll**

135

Always Welcome

There is something wondrous in the taste of bread. It is so ordinary yet it is so good. It is very democratic. It nourishes the poor and the rich. It goes well with meat or fish, with fruit or cheese. It may return three times a day to the table; it may even stay there all day long. Yet it never out-stays its welcome.

Ladislas M. Orsy

Alert to the Opportunity

When you seriously set yourself to seek for the truth, the truth brings into your life men and women who have different degrees of authentic knowledge and who are able to pass it on to you, if you are alert to the opportunity and willing to receive what is offered. You have to be on the lookout for these people. They do not appear ringing bells and waving flags. Their real nature is hidden from the reach of careless scrutiny. They do not lightly disclose themselves. You might know one of them quite inti-mately in an ordinary life situation, say that of a business associate or even a brother or sister, and yet not know him at all from a deeper stand-point.

Thomas E. Powers

Thinking in Chorus

Alice thought to herself 'Then there's no use in speaking.' The voices didn't join in, this time, as she hadn't spoken, but, to her great surprise, they all thought in chorus (I hope you understand what thinking in chorus means—for I must confess that I don't), 'Better say nothing at all. Language is worth a thousand pounds a word!'

Lewis Carroll

it means to each and all of us. As we pass it from hand to hand *(take the loaf and pass it around)* each of us imparts to the bread all that it means to him or her. As each of us breaks off a piece to eat, he or she takes into himself or herself part of all of us here.

We share in the bread, because we share in each other. We give, we receive, and the giving and receiving are the bonds that bind us together. Not only us, but each of us with the whole hu-man race. As you chew the bread very slowly and swallow it, allow this knowledge to permeate you, in this atmosphere of relaxation and mu-tuality.

(After everyone has completed the ritual, allow the members time to reflect. If there is bread left over, it may be returned to the center of the group. After the period of reflection is over, the leader concludes the exercise with words like the following.)

Carry the knowledge and the feelings that you have experienced here with you out into your everyday world; and realize that, even after the group has dispersed, a part of the group is still with you—and you, in turn, have given a part of yourself to every other member of the group.

Now I shall slowly count from one to three. When I reach three, blink your eyes three times. As soon as you have done this, you will be back in your usual reality state, feeling extremely well, physically and mentally.

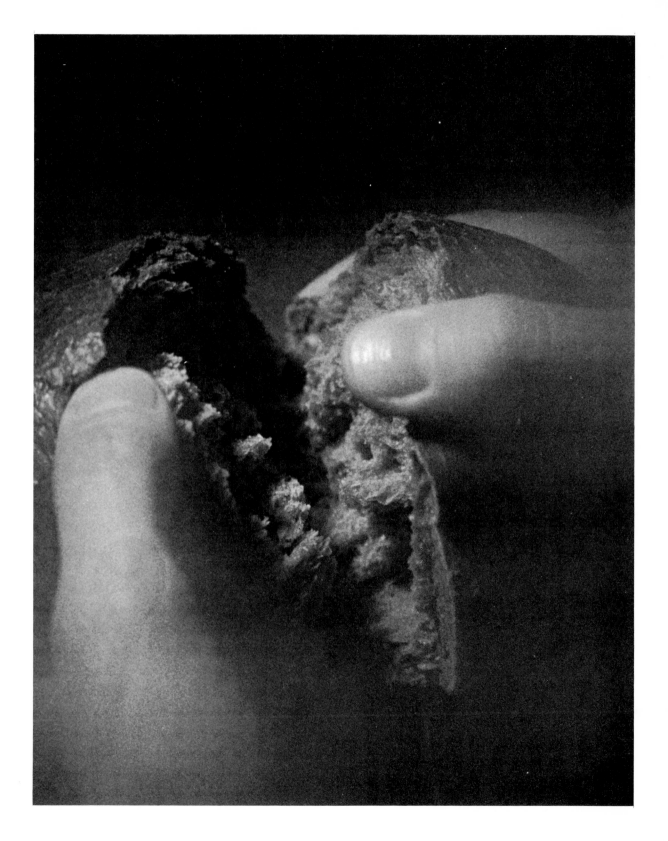

24.
Gemini

No matter what the specific purpose of the exercise in which trance-in-pairs is employed, the goal is always the enhancement of the experience through sharing. Trance-in-pairs is far more intimate than group trance; it is as if an extra dimension had been added to the privacy of solitary trance. In this intensification lies its value as well as its drawbacks and dangers.

The persons who enter into such a relationship should know and trust each other. They should both be level-headed people. During the exercise, their mutual involvement will be deep—possibly to the point of spontaneous telepathic rapport. If sensibly utilized, both parties can derive great benefit from it. Allow yourself to experience the shared relationship fully while it is happening; but be careful to terminate any special emotional involvement at the time of terminating the exercise, by incorporating the verbal safeguards given at the close of this exercise.

One more word of caution: Never let yourself be talked into a mutual trance relationship if you do not feel like going through with it; and never try to talk another person into it, no matter how valuable you think the association might be.

TIME
A long stretch of time should be available. Since two consciousnesses are involved and interacting, it is difficult to predict the direction the mind trip will take, or the time it will take to accomplish its purpose. It is a good idea to set aside a whole morning or whole afternoon.

INTRODUCTORY NOTE

So far we have dealt with only two basic personal settings for achieving altered states of consciousness: alone, and in groups.

There is a third variant for those who need the stimulation of another person's presence, yet find the group setting too public: seeking altered states of consciousness in pairs. The two participants may mutually induce an ASC, or utilize the help of a non-participating third person.

PREPARATION

If no outsider is involved, put yourselves into the trance state one at a time, by whatever method you usually use to achieve relaxation, but do it aloud, one after the other, addressing your unconscious mind in either the first or second person. Listening to the other person's "induction patter" will have a trance-inducing effect on the partner as well.

When you have both reached a light trance, deepen it by mutual induction. Say: "I will now count from ten to zero, and when I have reached zero you will be in a much deeper trance than at present." When that has been done, your partner should say: "Now I will count from ten to zero, and when I have reached zero, you will have joined me at this deeper level of consciousness where I am now waiting for you."

Both participants' trances can be considerably deepened by this technique.

THE EXERCISE

Choose a place, real or imaginary, where you wish to go in your mind, and tell your partner about it. If it is congenial to him or her, lead the way there, describing the landmarks en route in vivid detail, stopping or slowing down as necessary to enable your partner to keep in step. The companion may participate as fully as he wishes by asking questions, or even by incorporating his own details into the trip, if these are agreeable to you. Both participants should feel free to improvise.

You may go anywhere; your passage is not limited by the physical laws of time and space. In your

To See the Sunrise Together

Very often, I met Einstein at the exit from the Patent Office; sometimes we would take up the discussion we had left off the night before and sometimes we confided to others our hopes and fears. Our material situation was far from being brilliant; but, in spite of that, what enthusiasm we had, what fire, what a passion for the things that really mattered! We also made a number of excursions together—walking, sometimes climbing to the top of the Gurten Kulm on Saturday to see the sunrise. The scent of the pines, warmed by the sun during the day, used literally to intoxicate me.

Maurice Solovine

Merging

We swim together
in a clear pool of water
like two tadpoles
close to each other
face to face
ready to mate
and we stop swimming
and tread water
and the water slowly turns
blue blue blue
cerulean peacock blue
and slowly we too
turn the same blue
our arms our bodies
our necks and finally
our faces
and we merge with the water
into the water
and we merge with each other
into each other.

Anonymous

Four Visions

mind you may fly together to any part of the earth—or the universe. You may spin the calendar backward or forward through weeks or centuries to emerge clothed in the garments of another age.

Describe to each other the details along the way. Don't be in a hurry. If you see or hear or smell something your partner may have missed, point it out, and enjoy the richness of sharing. If you have a question about something, ask your partner about it. Share all your impulses.

Should you feel, or be told by your partner, that he cannot fully keep up with you, the difficulty may lie in a disparity of trance depths. Such imbalance should be corrected. Here is one way of testing your partner's depth:

140

Suggest to him that the numbers from ten to zero will now represent progressively deeper trance levels, zero being the deepest level; then request that he indicate his current level by telling you the first number that comes to his mind within this frame of reference.

Conclude the exercise by suggesting mutual awakening to reality by counting from one to three and opening your eyes; and suggest emphatically that this awakening will coincide with complete cessation of any special emotional involvement induced by the shared experience.

The First Fruits of Growing

One person helps the other to new discoveries. In this atmosphere of peace many more shutters can be opened. Seeing a person, one senses more of what is going on in him. The fine movements of breathing, his expression, the whole language of his body begins to speak. In this non-verbal communication, the coming more in touch without actual touching is the first fruit of growing quiet and sensitive.

Charlotte Selver

25.

Body Laser

In the context of Passages, "scanning" a person denotes a process designed to answer two questions: "How is he?" and "How does he feel?" The first question has an almost purely physical connotation; the second may refer to physical or emotional factors, or to a combination of both. The following two exercises deal with each of these two forms of scanning.

Try them first with someone to whom you feel close; the motivational force of personal interest may well make the difference between success and failure. With practice, you will become sufficiently proficient to scan a person effectively even when your emotions are not engaged.

PREPARATION

GOAL
To discover the state of health of another person.

TIME
Approximately 30 minutes.

Sit down opposite the person you are planning to scan and put yourself into an altered state of consciousness by focusing your eyes on the other person's forehead until your eyes tire and close. While retaining the after-image of the person's face behind your closed lids, count from ten to zero, and tell yourself that on reaching zero you will be in a deep state of trance.

142

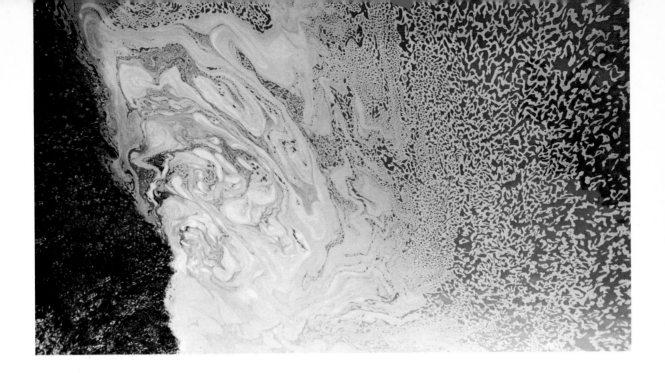

THE EXERCISE

Now that you have reached effective trance depth, focus your mind's eye sharply on your partner's whole figure, striving to see it as clearly as you saw his face when your eyes were open. Hold on to this sharply etched image for a moment.

Now tell yourself that you will count from one to three, and when you have reached three, your mind will begin to penetrate the surface of this figure-image you hold in your mind's eye, penetrate steadily, deeper and deeper, like a laser beam, imperceptibly but inexorably. And as it penetrates deeper and deeper, this benevolent, painless laser beam will begin to shed light on the inner body of your partner, revealing his skeletal frame, his circulatory and digestive systems, his muscles, nerves, and organs.

Scan his entire body in this manner—head, shoulders, arms, chest, stomach, digestive system, legs and feet—skimming swiftly but lightly and carefully, like a caress.

Having done this, stop a moment to allow your deeper mind to absorb the information.

A Strange Talent

As a child, Edgar Cayce displayed powers of perception that seemed to extend beyond the normal range of the five senses. At the age of six or seven he told his parents that he was able to see and talk to "visions," sometimes of relatives who had recently died. His parents attributed this phenomenon to the overactive imagination of a lonely child influenced by the dramatic language of the revival meetings that were popular in that section of the country.

By the time he was in his early twenties, Edgar's unique abilities as a medical diagnostician while in a state of self-induced trance became widely known. A group of physicians from Hopkinsville and Bowling Green, Kentucky, took advantage of his strange talent to diagnose their own patients. They soon discovered that Edgar only needed to be given the name and address of a patient, wherever he was, to be able to "tune in" telepathically on that individual's mind and body as easily as though both he and the patient were in the same room. He did not need, and was not given, any other information regarding the patient.

August H. Wagner

Scanning

One is asked to concentrate on scanning a certain area of one's body and to combine this with one's inhalation. Gradually the two tasks will connect, as if one were breathing with that particular area, or being breathed by it.

Magda Proskauer

A Receptive Onlooker

The conscious exercises of attention lead to a spontaneous flow of experience to which the person becomes a receptive onlooker—extreme, separate self is lost and union with the object of meditation is felt.

Edward Maupin

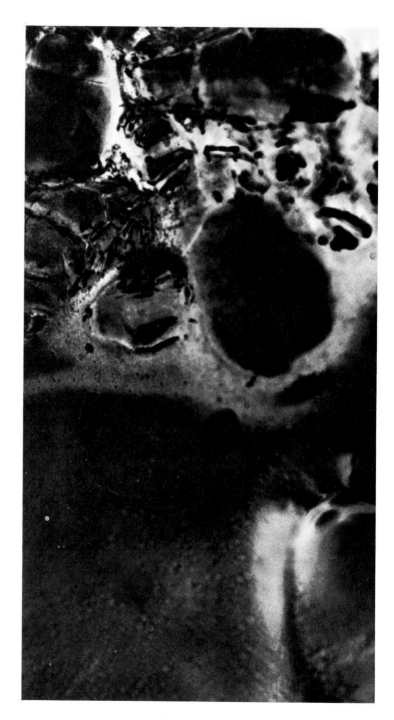

Then, tell yourself that you will again count from one to three; and when you have reached three, your mind will point out to you any trouble spot there may be in this body you have scanned, by focusing the laser beam on that spot, setting it off sharply from the surrounding darkness. Allow yourself time to focus. There is no need to hurry. Perhaps there is no perceptible trouble in the person's body, and the light will not settle anywhere. Or perhaps the problem is not clearly localized. But, at times, your mind will point out to you a particular trouble spot by clearly focusing the laser beam on it.

In either case, do not attempt medical diagnosis of any kind. Your function is to use your ability for the good of your partner by pointing out an area which may require medical attention. Your task is to locate the area, not to perform medical functions.

You may see such a potential trouble spot in a number of ways, but you are most likely to see it as an area of different, darker color, or slightly more prominent than the rest.

When you have completed the scan, tell yourself that you will count from one to three and open your eyes. As soon as you have opened them you will be back in your normal reality state, feeling relaxed and at ease, ready to use the information your deeper mind has given you to your partner's best advantage.

NOTE

Be sure to remember that no medical knowledge or ability whatever has been conferred on you. You may, for instance, see a darkened area in the center of your partner's chest cavity. This may denote conditions as disparate as influenza, pharyngitis, emphysema, bronchial asthma, or the remnants of last week's cold. It is not for you to state which it is, even if you feel you know.

**Nothing Wrong,
Something the Matter**

His body is hurting him so he goes to a doctor. And supposing the affection is as yet "merely functional," that is, there are not yet any gross anatomical or physiological ravages: the doctor decides there is nothing wrong with him and gives him aspirin. For the doctor too believes that the body is an affectless physiological system. Great institutions of learning are founded on the proposition that there are a body and a mind. It is estimated that more than 60% of visitors to medical offices have nothing the matter with them; but they obviously have something the matter with them.

Paul Goodman

145

26.

Currents

INTRODUCTORY NOTE

People are continually providing clues—in their behavior, posture, movement, voice—which help you to know how they feel. To make full use of these explicit and subliminal clues, it helps to be in an altered state of consciousness with eyes open. If you find this too difficult to achieve the first few times you attempt this exercise, study your partner as closely as you did in the preceding exercise, then enter an altered state with your eyes closed, and retain his after-image while deepening your trance.

PREPARATION

Sit in a comfortable chair opposite your partner, with your hands on your lap, and focus your eyes on an imaginary point in the center of his forehead. Try not to blink. When your vision begins to blur, tell yourself that you will now count from ten to zero, and that, on reaching zero, you will be in your altered state of consciousness, with your eyes still open and feeling no fatigue. From this point on, you need no longer keep yourself from blinking.

GOAL
To discover the mental or emotional state of another person.

TIME
Approximately 30 minutes.

THE EXERCISE

You are in your trance state now, your eyes focused comfortably on your partner's forehead. Tell yourself that you will count from one to three. On reaching three, you will become aware of any clues to his state of mind which his appearance may have given you subliminally during the preceding minutes. Suggest to yourself that you will clearly recall such clues as expression of the eyes, timbre of the voice, signs of restlessness or repose, quick, shallow breathing or slow, deep breathing. If your mind registers any such details remind yourself to store them for subsequent reference.

Now tell yourself that you will count from one to three again, and as you count, your eyes will begin to penetrate deeper and deeper into your partner's forehead, deeper and deeper and deeper, until you are with him inside his head, inside his thoughts. Do not grope or intellectualize; let yourself be led by your trance-focused mind. Relax and observe while you look at him from the inside.

Tuned-in

Even as radio waves are picked up wherever a set is tuned-in to their wave-length, so the thoughts which each of us think each moment of the day go forth into the world to influence for good or bad each other human mind.

Christmas Humphreys

The Bonds Between Us

Nothing can fill the gap when we are away from those we love, and it would be wrong to try and find anything. We must simply hold out and win through. That sounds very hard at first, but at the same time it is a great consolation, since leaving the gap unfilled preserves the bonds between us. It is nonsense to say that God fills the gap; he does not fill it, but keeps it empty so that our communion with another may be kept alive, even at the cost of pain.

Dietrich Bonhoeffer

147

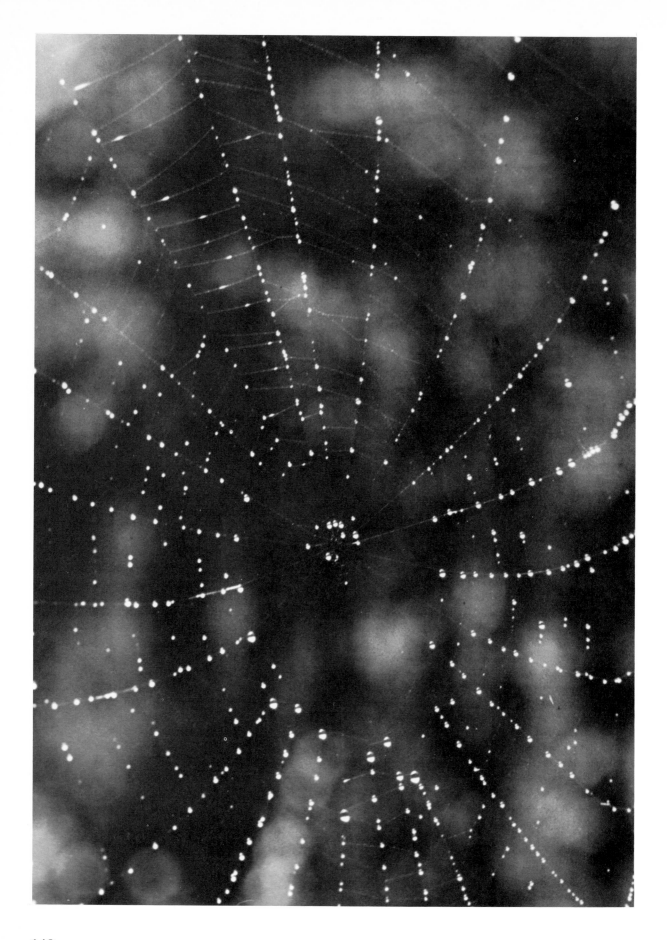

And now, imagine that thin, golden strands are beginning to grow out of your fingertips, infinitely graceful and delicate strands, growing and growing, until they reach your partner's fingertips and gently, painlessly, attach themselves there, as if they had found their natural home. Now you and your partner are connected; you are truly one— the substance of one joined to that of the other, current flowing back and forth between you in a closed circuit excluding all others. There is no need to grope for thoughts and impressions; it is only necessary to wait, receptively, for the information to travel down that fragile golden route until it reaches you.

Soon, very soon now, you will become aware of a mood, a quality of thought. Recall any subliminal details you may have identified a few minutes ago, and try to incorporate them into this mood easily, without forcing. Ask yourself: Do the mood and the details dovetail?

Do not aim for specific information, for precise thought content. Just let your partner's mood pervade you until it becomes your own, until you *feel* his apprehension or anticipation, doubt or certainty, joy or sorrow, anger or elation. In time, if you are very gifted, specific thoughts may occasionally be revealed to you, but these will most likely come spontaneously. Accept them as they come: Don't reject them, don't command them, don't try to modify or interpret them.

Continue to feel your partner's mood throughout your own self, to share it as a participant rather than as an onlooker. Fill your mind with the wish to be helpful to him, if his mood seems to require this, if you feel that he is in need of help in any form. If he is happy and joyful, rejoice with him in his happiness. Strive for that completeness of empathy which lies beyond sympathy.

When you are ready to end the exercise, tell yourself that you will count from one to three and then blink your eyes three times. As soon as you have blinked for the third time, you will be back in your ordinary reality state, a self-contained entity again, feeling relaxed and at ease, and filled with a new and deep understanding of your partner.

To Spot Somebody

I remember reading years ago a little tract written by Frank Laubach, a great man of prayer, in which he described one of his prayer practices. When he is on a journey, even on a streetcar going a few blocks, he tries to spot somebody on the car who seems to him to be in distress, or perhaps just tired or lonely, and to direct his prayers toward that person as though the Divine possession were streaming out from him to this other person. This I believe to be the essence of the Christian life: that we act as purveyors of the very Spirit of God Himself to the world around us.

H. L. Puxley

Profound Alterations

There are psychological states for which there are no good names, including feeling states, cognitive states and volitional states, upon which human destiny almost literally may depend, with resulting understanding of those profound alterations in states of consciousness, well known to the East, regarding which Western man usually has expressed doubt or scorn.

Gardner Murphy

27.

In the Wake of the Dolphin

INTRODUCTORY NOTE

The primary reason for performing this exercise in an altered state of consciousness is to facilitate the mind's acceptance of an unusual milieu. It will therefore be wise to try it first while you are in an easy-going, receptive mood, not harried by the need to solve a specific problem. The closer you can approximate reverie conditions, the better.

PREPARATION

GOAL

To learn to experience extra-human states of being.

TIME
Approximately 30 minutes

Lying in bed before going to sleep, turn off the light and close your eyes. Relax your whole body, going deeper and deeper, while you mentally follow the ebbing of tension in muscle after muscle. When relaxation has spread throughout your body, from the top of your head to the tips of your toes, from your shoulders to your fingertips, tell yourself that you will slowly count from ten to zero, visualizing each number as you count; and that, on reaching zero, you will have reached a much deeper level of consciousness.

THE EXERCISE

You have now arrived at this deeper level, enabling your mind to expand, so that you can formulate and accept novel concepts. See yourself in a large, open-air swimming pool in beautiful surroundings, comfortably immersed in water of exactly the right temperature, carried by the soothing motion of waves, listening to their gentle, rippling sound. The bed of waves supports you securely and surrounds you lovingly, extending far in all directions, farther and farther, beyond the horizon—until it becomes an endless ocean without shoreline. There is nothing to break the continuity of support and the rhythm of sound.

You feel the need to share this delightful experience with someone; and as soon as you have formulated the thought, you find yourself part of an aquatic ballet. To your delight, you find that your body is completely at ease performing the intricate routines and succession of configurations, which seem at once so spontaneous and yet so familiar.

Your motions synchronize effortlessly with those of the others. Now you find yourself at the bottom of the ocean with them, and slowly, gracefully you rise with them, easily following the tempo and rhythm of your companions. A great feeling of joy and well-being fills you at this perfectly executed group maneuver. You want to be part of it again, to experience that sense of accomplishment and well-being again. And so you begin again.

But now there is a slight difficulty: diving toward the bottom is more difficult than rising from it. Your movements are not as fluid, not as graceful. The water resists your descent, and it is not as clear as it was, so that you are not quite sure of the direction in which you are to move. In fact, the water is becoming viscous and murky; somehow you must clear it, to see where you are going. If only you had someone to guide you!

The moment you become aware of the need, it is filled: a dolphin appears to show you the way.

Understanding Creation

I could see nothing but the sea. The waves rolled up the shingle to my feet, foamed on the rocks at water level, broke on them in cadence, embraced them like watery arms, like lucent veils, and fell back transfused with blue. The wind blew the spume around me and wrinkled the surface of the pools left behind in the crevices; the seaweed swayed and dripped, still rocked by the motion of the retreating wave . . . As the sea retreated and its sound grew more distant, like a dying refrain, the beach advanced toward me, discovering the furrows traced by waves on the sand. And then I understood all the happiness of creation, all the joy with which God has endowed it for man.

Gustave Flaubert

Seeing the Unity

Who sees variety and not the unity wanders on from death to death.

The Upanishads

151

Crossing a Frontier

Whether one walks, rides a camel, flies, or dives deep into the sea, it is for the sole purpose of crossing a frontier beyond which man ceases to feel himself the master, sure of his techniques, upheld by his inheritance, backed by the crowd. The more powerless he is, the more his spirit permeates his being. The horizon of the world and the horizon of thought coincide within him. Then the water, the rocks and the sand become vital nourishment, and perhaps a poem.

Philippe Diolé

The Most Reliable Sources

In sensing, the person will meet consciously for the first time the creative, self-directive powers of his own nature, finding that he can orient himself where he formerly used to seek advice and that his most reliable sources of information and guidance lie within him.

Charlotte Selver

Everything in this private ocean of yours is so right, so inevitable, that you are not even startled. After all, the dolphin is the most intelligent of the sea's creatures; intelligent enough to have a language, to communicate—even to understand the unreasonable demands of man. And if man cannot always understand the dolphin's language, it is the fault of man, not of the dolphin.

But you do understand. You communicate perfectly with him, because you have become aware of another certainty in this wondrous ocean: Language and communication need not depend on words. Without audible sound to inform him, the dolphin knows that you need a guide; without spoken reassurance, you know that you can trust him, that he will guide you well, wherever he chooses to lead.

He swims ahead of you and you follow, knowing that all is well. Only—he is so very big, and, swimming ahead of you, he obscures your whole field of vision. And everything here is so interesting that the thought of missing any of it makes you a little impatient with his bulk. You say nothing because you like the dolphin, but suddenly you know that he knows: his radar has picked up your impatience.

And now he puts on a magnificent display for you: without any break in his graceful glide ahead of you he answers your thought by means of tracings emanating from the radar in his head. His tracings are a beautiful kaleidoscope of ever-changing designs, each representing an answering word. Only they are lost on you, because you cannot understand his language as yet. All you can make out are patterns of inscrutable arabesques.

If only there were a way to learn this language, if only one could discover what is in his head. . . . That's it! You have found the answer: to give meaning to the arabesques, you must pursue them to their source; you must project yourself into the dolphin's head, so that his sensing devices will be yours as well, so that the language of his arabesques will be as clear to you as it is to him and his kind.

See and feel yourself moving forward, gaining on him slowly, drawing alongside him, closer and closer, until your outlines blur and merge, until you are inside his head, until he is part of you and you of him, and you understand his language and his thoughts as you do your own. Spend some time within the dolphin. Study his feelings, his language as long as you wish.

When you have finished your explorations, tell yourself that you will count from one to five, and with each count you will withdraw a little from the dolphin's head and he will become a little more remote, until, at the count of five, you will have assumed your separate identity again and the dolphin will have vanished. Now tell yourself that you will shortly count from one to three, and after the count of three you will open your eyes. As soon as you open them you will be back in your ordinary state of mind, feeling very comfortable, very relaxed, and greatly enriched by your adventure of the mind.

28.
Double Vision

INTRODUCTORY NOTE

Empathy in an altered state of consciousness is infinitely more extensive and intensive than empathy in the ordinary waking state. When experienced in a joint trance with a close friend, it may be intense enough to engender flashes of ESP.

The following exercise presents a hypothetical sample of the kind of phenomena that may be encountered when the powerful strands of empathy and non-ordinary consciousness are interwoven. Use the sample story as a guide when adapting the exercise to your own experiences.

PREPARATION

First, decide which of the two partners will act as leader during the common journey backward in time. Then, with eyes closed, you may enter your altered state of consciousness either separately, or induce and deepen it in mutual cooperation, using suggestions of relaxation and counts from ten to zero.

THE EXERCISE

GOAL

To achieve new depths of empathy with another human being, by means of joint age regression.

TIME
30-45 minutes.

You have now both attained a medium-deep trance. If you are the leader, suggest to your partner that he is about to see an image of himself in his current state, and that this image will presently begin to recede—in time, rather than in distance or size. Allow a few moments to elapse, while you, too, evoke an image of your partner behind your closed lids, and try, in a relaxed way, to follow its progressive changes of appearance as he grows younger.

Suggest to your partner that his present self and the self of his image are gradually merging; that he is actually going back in time—back, back, and still further back, all the way back to childhood. Ask him to stop and let you know when he has reached his ten-year-old self. When he so informs you, the picture behind your own eyes will also be that of your partner at the age of ten.

Now ask him to choose a day in any month of that year—the first date that comes to his mind. When he has selected it, ask him for details, seeing each fragment of information take shape as you hear it spoken. Did anything particular happen on that day?

Yes, he may tell you; he had an accident. "A bicycling accident . . . I'm riding down a country lane, and it gets steeper and steeper . . . It was fun at first but now it's scary . . . I want to stop but I can't, and here's that sharp curve—ooohhh . . ."

Behind your closed lids you have been following this ride as if it were your own, feeling the gathering momentum, the mounting panic. *Your* hands are gripping the handle-bars, *your* feet are trying vainly to brake as you hurtle down the road, and every inch of you feels the jarring impact of the fall, even before your mind sees the ten-year-old body sprawled on the road.

You hear sobbing, and your partner tells you where it hurts: both knees are bloody, and there is a burning sensation on the palm of his hand.

You tell him to examine himself, to see what is wrong. "My knees—they're all bloody. There are stones and pebbles around here, and they're sharp, and my hand hurts so. There's this deep gash—that hurts worst, and it's swollen."

Suggest to him that he will now rest and relax; that, although it is still the day of the accident, he will no longer be frightened, and his hand will no

A Particular State of Mind

The occurrence of ESP is not determined by being an extraordinary gifted individual, but rather by attaining a specific state of mind. Its rare occurrence can be explained by the fact that only few individuals attain this particular state of mind—whatever may be the reason.

Milan Ryzl

Your Face or my Face

Sometimes I would have a hard time telling whether your face was your face or whether I was there—rather than that it was myself, rather than any extension or anything else—just merely the self in the same way as any other part of oneself. In many ways there was kind of a relaxing feeling, almost like being asleep for three years.

Paul Bindrim

Capacity to Empathize

This capacity for consciousness of ourselves gives us the ability to see ourselves as others see us and to have empathy with others. It underlies our remarkable capacity to transport ourselves into someone else's parlor where we will be in reality next week, and then in imagination to think and plan how we will act. And it enables us to imagine ourselves in someone else's place, and to ask how we would feel and what we would do if we were this other person. No matter how poorly we use or fail to use or even abuse these capacities, they are the rudiments of our ability to begin to love our neighbor, to have ethical sensitivity, to see truth, to create beauty, to devote ourselves to ideals, and to die for them if need be.

To fulfill these potentialities is to be a person.

Rollo May

In You Everybody

If I truly love one person, I love all persons, I love the world, I love life. If I can say to somebody else, "I love you," I must be able to say, "I love in you everybody. I love through you the world, I love in you also myself."

Erich Fromm

We Dare Not go A-hunting

Polite how are you,
Weather and health report
Are pleasant punctuation
To routine everyday;
I like the cheerful
Grunts and sneezes
Punctuating everyday,
But I hunger for
The deeper satisfaction
Of exploring; I must stop
Looking for someone
To go with me —
Or I'll never go . . .

Ione Hill

Creative Needs

. . . for the ego is a dream
Till a neighbor's need by name
    create it.

W. H. Auden

A Two-way Flow

We must assume that there is a well-nigh unlimited two-way flow of mental content passing between parent and child, and at this stage (i.e., the pre-verbal), telepathy serves a compelling biological need and represents a functional link between mother and child here and now, comparable to the function of instinct which, according to current concepts, forms the connecting link between successive generations in the longitudinal section of our racial history.

J. Ehrenwald

longer hurt. There is a shield between him and the fear and the pain.

But you continue concentrating on his hand, and suddenly you know beyond all doubt that it is the left one. You know this as surely as if it were your own . . . it *is* your own. You touch the palm of your left hand, and feel a slight lump. At once your inner eyes see it, and while you inspect it you feel it becoming more prominent, redder, and harder. You have incorporated this small angry inflamed lump into your hand; and as you continue to study it, your inner eye suddenly sees beneath the surface of the skin and you discover the cause of the lump: a pebble has become lodged there, and scar tissue has formed over it.

Now you tell your partner that he will stay completely relaxed and at ease while he picks another date, again the first one that comes to mind. What happened on that date?

"That's when the doctor cut my hand open and took the pebble out—the pebble that had got stuck there. It hurt when he pushed the needle in, and then I didn't feel anything . . . "

This second experience, like the first, reverberates in you as if it were your own. You live two sets of experiences—your partner's and your own. And through this process of feeling and knowing on two levels, your perceptions are immeasurably sharpened. It is as if a long-dormant part of you had been awakened, never to fall entirely asleep again.

And now, before you count from one to three and open your eyes, suggest that, as soon as you open them, you will both have returned completely to your customary reality state, feeling very relaxed and in excellent health, and very close to each other as a result of this shared journey.

*   *   *

Remember that this was a hypothetical sample. It will guide you in your responses to whatever material emerges when you perform the exercise.

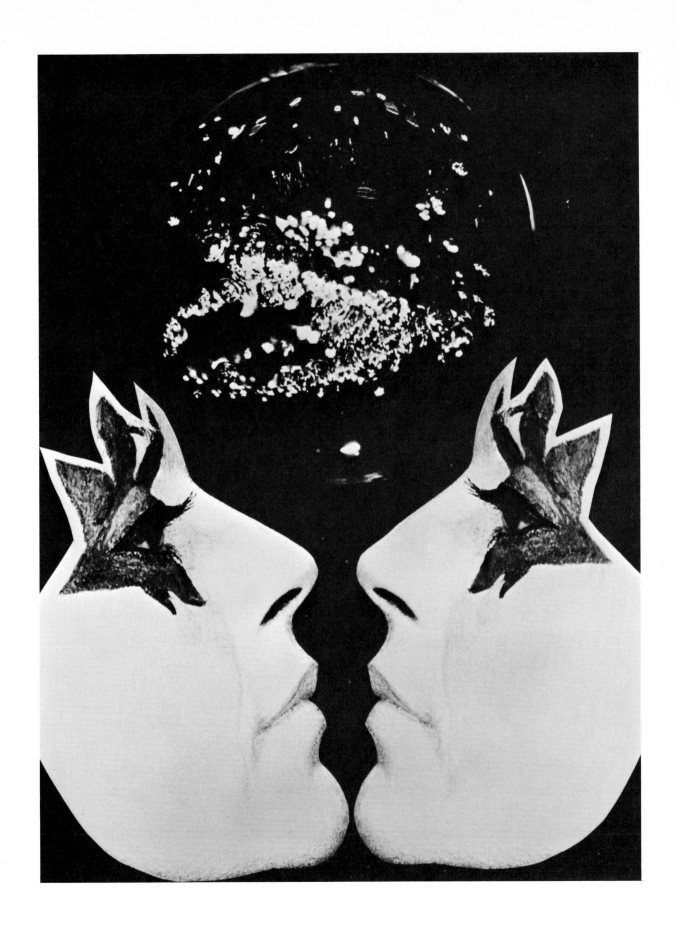

29.

Elemental Rhythms

INTRODUCTORY NOTE

Music is an effective stimulus and complement to many activities in altered states of consciousness. People who have experienced altered states with and without music strongly prefer music to be a part of their experiences.

Music supports the altered states experience by providing a special kind of emotional continuity, and by enriching it in interrelated ways: (1) It helps individuals relinquish their controls and enter more fully into their own inner world; (2) It facilitates the release of intense feelings where strong emotions are involved; and (3) it contributes toward peak experiences.

For these reasons, it is often helpful to program music to accompany your experience in altered states of consciousness. Your favorite music is not necessarily the best choice; selections should be chosen for their ability to facilitate and enhance the experience and feel of each exercise.

GOAL
To enjoy and maintain inner peace and contentment through music.

The following selections have been found to be especially effective: *In A Summer Garden*, by Delius, Angel S-36588; Beethoven's *Sixth Symphony* (Pastoral), Movements I and II, MS 6549; and *In Search of the Lost Chord*, Moody Blues, "Visions of Paradise," DES 18017 (or all of side 2 for longer sessions).

You may play the music on an ordinary speaker system, but the strongest effects are experienced when the music is listened to through head phones.

TIME
Half an hour or more.

PREPARATION

Using a favorite relaxation technique, close your eyes, and self-induce an altered state of consciousness.

THE EXERCISE

When you have reached a deeper level of mind, suggest to yourself that you are seated in a summer meadow, near a brook, under a shady tree. It is vacation time and you are completely free. All your responsibilities have been put aside for the moment; for once, you are free to relax and simply *be*. The peace of the meadow fills you. You hear the sounds of nature, the bubbling water, the rustling leaves, the humming of insects, but you have a deeper desire: You wish that the meadow could communicate its meaning to you much more deeply, that it would invite you inside its own experience, letting you share its feelings.

(At this point begin the music.)

Deepen your altered state by counting from five to one, so that you may be deep enough to hear what nature wants to say to you. Let the music take you to places where you have never been, let the sounds show you deeper levels of consciousness than you have ever experienced—the peace and contentment and joy that nature knows in its elemental rhythms.

Stay with the musical experience as long as you like, stopping the record at any point or letting it play until the end.

Periods for Expression

If our sanity is to be strong and flexible, there must be occasional periods for the expression of completely spontaneous movement—for dancing, singing, howling, babbling, jumping, groaning, wailing—in short, for following any motion to which the organism as a whole seems to be inclined. It is by no means impossible to set up physical and moral boundaries within which this freedom of action is expressible—sensible contexts in which nonsense may have its way.

Alan Watts

Dancing Waves

We have but to stand on the seashore and watch the waves that beat at our feet, to observe that at nearly regular intervals this seemingly monotonous rhythm is accentuated for several beats, so that the waves are really dancing the measure of a tune.

Havelock Ellis

In Every Moment of Listening

No one imagines that a symphony is supposed to improve in quality as it goes along, or that the whole object of playing it is to reach the finale. The point of music is discovered in every moment of playing and listening to it. It is the same, I feel, with the greater part of our lives, and if we are unduly absorbed in improving them we may forget altogether to live them.

Alan Watts

Without Music

Without music
life would be a mistake.

Friedrich Nietzsche

In Rhythm With the Music

There was an experience which culminated in a nothingness—just a beating of my chest in time to the music. It may have been Scriabin's Poem of Ecstasy. Pressure building up in rhythm with the music, I could feel myself taking six deep inspirations as though the music was pacing my respirations. It was a sublime feeling of not being able to get enough of this beautiful music inside me. Filling up to the bursting point at the time that the music subsided, I felt like I was floating down—exhausted.

Patient in a music therapy session reported by Helen L. Bonny

Everything Fit Together

I had a feeling that everything in the Universe fit together and there was some sort of higher order to everything. I vaguely remember some kind of majestic music playing at this point.

Patient in a music therapy session reported by Helen L. Bonny

To Unite With the Universe

A person going through such a musical experience may feel as if the limits of his ego dissolve and as if he is about to unite with the universe, and even to master it.

P. Noy

When you are ready to return to normal consciousness, tell yourself that after you count one-two-three, you will open your eyes and be back in your usual reality state, feeling deeply at peace, happy to discover new places to explore with the help of music, and planning to return here again to uncover within you ever deeper levels of inner joy and peace.

ADDITIONAL SUGGESTIONS

The following selections are samples of musical recordings which have been found effective in evoking moods or settings in altered states of consciousness:

Recording	Mood or Setting
Montovani: **Songs to Remember** PS 193 London	sentimental—evocative of the security of the good old days.
Vivaldi: **Concerto in D, Guitar** CM 9270	quiet, soothing predictability
Ralph Vaugh Williams: **Fantasia on Greensleeves** Angel 36101	quiet, contemplation of nature
Beethoven: **Piano Concerto #5;** Adagio BC 1139	exquisite simplicity of continuity in the melodic line; built on the strong supportive base of the orchestra
Grofe: **Grand Canyon Suite,** Sunrise, SDBR 3044	majestic; breaking through barriers; vigorous
Simon & Garfunkel: **Bridge Over Troubled Waters,** KCS 9914	triumph of human spirit; confidence
John Coltrane: **A Love Supreme** LIP A-77 (band 1, side 1)	melancholy, doleful, sober
Debussy: **Girl with the Flaxen Hair, Sunken Cathedral** Time-Life	fragile loveliness; depth of feeling related to cosmic consciousness
Mahalia Jackson: **I Believe** CS 1549	motherhood—Mother Earth—security

The Creative Composer

The question is, "Do you compose at the piano, or at a desk, or where?" Well, the answer to that is that I sometimes do compose at the piano, and sometimes at a desk, and sometimes in airports, and sometimes walking down the street; but mostly I compose in bed, lying down, or on a sofa, lying down. I should think that most composing by almost any composer happens lying down. Many a time my wife has walked into my studio and found me lying down and has said, "Oh, I thought you were working, excuse me!" And I was working, but you'd never have known it.

Now, this is a kind of trance state, I suppose, which doesn't exactly sound like a very ideal condition for working, but rather a condition for contemplating, but there is a very strong relation between creative work and contemplation . . .

As you lie on a bed or on the floor or wherever, and the conscious mind becomes hazier and hazier, the level of consciousness begins to lower, so that you find yourself somewhere at the borderland of this twilight area, which is the area, let's say, wherein fantasies occur at night when you're falling asleep.

Everybody has that experience whether he's creative or not . . . That's kind of the moment you want. And if the fantasy happens to be a creative one, if it happens to be taking place in terms of notes, or, if you're a writer or painter, in terms of words or design—in other words, if it is a creative vision you are having and you are still awake enough to remember it and appreciate it and know how to go about making it permanent (that is, when you arrive back in consciousness to formulate the vision into something communicable to other people)—then I suppose you've hit the ideal state.

Leonard Bernstein

161

TRANSCENDING

30.
A Thousand Eyes

GOAL
To enhance creativity and awareness by exploring the many meanings to be found in a photograph.

TIME
30-45 minutes.

PREPARATION

Read through this entire exercise in your normal waking state, to familiarize yourself with the process. Before you enter an altered state of consciousness, look at the accompanying photograph, and allow yourself to feel its mood and impact. Then create *your own* background story to explain the meaning of the photograph. Then begin the exercise.

THE EXERCISE

Put yourself into a fairly deep trance by whatever method fits your present mood.

When you have reached your altered state of consciousness, set to work on inventing new

164

"stories" that fit the visible facts in the photograph. Here are two examples of stories that fit the facts.

Let's suppose your first impression of the photograph is favorable—an impression of a vacationer, far from the madding crowd, relaxing on a summer day at a quiet beach. He has been lying there peacefully for some time, burrowing into the sand with his feet, idly pushing it into little mounds around his upturned heels, wiggling his toes in the seaweed, liking the feel of the streamers against his skin. But he realizes that the tide is returning, and that he must soon abandon this blissful state of drowsiness. The sound of the lapping waves is becoming louder and more insistent. Lazily he wonders how long it will be before the water reaches him. . . .

Now you look at the photograph again, and suddenly you are amazed that its menacing quality

Travel

I should like to rise and go
Where the golden apples grow; —
Where below another sky
Parrot islands anchored lie,
And, watched by cockatoos
   and goats,
Lonely Crusoes building boats . . .

        Robert Louis Stevenson

Doors of Perception

If the doors of perception were cleansed, man would see things as they are, infinite.

        William Blake

had eluded you before. What, you wonder, made you so sure there's man there? The evidence of the photograph reveals only a stark, abandoned beach and a pair of abandoned feet. Perhaps the feet have been there so long that the seaweed has covered them, and the tide has come and gone so often that it has shaped the sand into graves around them. With each ebb and flow of the tide the graves grow deeper; soon the feet will disappear, and there will be only sand and seaweed . . .

NOTE

Whatever impression you follow in your altered state of consciousness, do not let your mind drift. Give your imagination sufficient leeway to choose the point of departure; but from that moment on, bring your thoughts gently back into line whenever they show a tendency to wander.

You will find that in your altered state of consciousness you not only command a greater range and fluidity of imagination; your powers of concentration are equally enhanced, and will permit you to focus more and more accurately on whatever point of interest you choose.

When you are ready to conclude the exercise, tell yourself that you will count from one to three and then open your eyes. As soon as you have opened them you will be back in your customary reality state, feeling extremely well, relaxed, and at ease, and feeling also an enhanced sense of creativity within you.

The Presence of Thoughts

I have also realized that one must accept the thoughts that go on within oneself of their own accord as part of one's reality. The categories of true and false are, of course, always present; but because they are not binding they take second place. The presence of thoughts is more important than our subjective judgment of them. But neither must these judgments be suppressed, for they also are existent thoughts which are part of our wholeness.

C. C. Jung

Looking at Photographs

Photographs of family members often are a rich source of personal insight. They seem to come to life, often with the appearance they had at some significant past point in time, and relationships may be seen with extraordinary clarity as in the following examples:

"I looked at several pictures and then at one of my father—a stern steely looking one. The feeling immediately overwhelmed me. A heavy hand fell on my neck and a pain pierced my left eye. I said, 'That's what it is—those eyes. I'm dead when he looks at me. He's killed all the feeling in me . . . I feel it, the shutting down, the dullness . . . He never liked me . . .'"

Willis W. Harman

31.

Fata Morgana

GOAL

Sometimes creativity flows smoothly and effortlessly within an individual, sometimes it needs a nudge. This exercise may serve as a nudge whenever the need arises.

TIME

Allow approximately 30 minutes.

PREPARATION

Settle down in a comfortable armchair, facing a low-watt, soft-light lamp. Look at the light steadily while you enter your altered state of consciousness by means of relaxation suggestions and a count from ten to zero.

THE EXERCISE

Keep your eyes fixed on the light. It is bright enough to hold your attention, and soft enough to enhance your relaxation. Let your eyes and your mind slowly absorb the light of the lamp, then close your eyes, and behind your closed lids see the after-image left by the light. It will be different every time you engage in this exercise; and every time it will help you to find your creative self.

Today the after-image of the light swirls like a thick, white mist. Watch the dance of the mist as it billows, ebbs, and flows in continuous movement, weaving silent arabesques.

You walk into the mist and feel it cling all around you, enfolding you in a soft, white embrace. Then, slowly, the mist begins to dissolve as the warm sun penetrates it. As the mist slowly dissipates, other forms emerge and you find yourself walking in a pine forest. Pine needles make a firm, springy carpet beneath your feet. You reach out to feel the rough bark of the trees that tower above you. The scent of pine fills the clean, cold air. The sun shines warm through the last wisps of mist and through the dark green pine branches, and lights up the forest with cool, green shade.

Stand for a moment and watch the light weave dappled patterns on the forest floor as the sun's beams glint and sparkle through the trees.

The Magic Power

No sooner had I decided to give up my poetry and closed my mouth than a sentiment tempted my heart and something flickered in my mind. Such is the magic power of the poetic spirit.

Basho

In Thy Heart

Thus, great with child to speak,
and helpless in my throes,
Biting my truant pen,
beating myself for spite;
"Fool," said my Muse to me,
"look in thy heart, and write!"

**From Astrophel and Stella
Sir Philip Sidney**

Capable of New Energy

It is a secret which every intellectual man quickly learns, that beyond the energy of his possessed and conscious intellect he is capable of a new energy (as of an intellect doubled on itself), by abandonment to the nature of things; that beside his privacy of power as an individual man, there is a great public power on which he can draw, by unlocking, at all risks, his human doors, and suffering the ethereal tides to roll and circulate through him; then he is caught up into the life of the Universe, his speech is thunder, his thought is law, and his words are universally intelligible as the plants and animals. The poet knows that he speaks adequately then only when he speaks somewhat wildly, or "with the flower of the mind"; not with the intellect used as an organ, but with the intellect released from all service and suffered to take its direction from its celestial life . . .

Ralph Waldo Emerson

In a Transcendental Language

A line, a shade, a color—
their fiery expressiveness.

The language of flowers,
mountains, shores,
human bodies:
the interplay of light and shade
in a look,
the aching beauty of a neckline,
the grail of the white crocus
on the alpine meadow
in the morning sunshine—
words in a transcendental
language of the senses.

Dag Hammarskjöld

Stillness fills the air. As you wander along the rough track through the trees, that stillness becomes a sound—music. Listen carefully and let the music guide you. The path opens out into a clearing, and there is the source of your music: A gypsy sitting by his caravan, playing a violin. The smoke from his fire spirals up with the notes that flow from his supple fingers. You stop and hold your breath. He is playing the solo part of a violin concerto, and you feel on the brink of a new, unique experience: You are about to see music.

Here is the pause that heralds the cadenza. And now, a silver streak of sound arises in a shimmering spiral, returns to meet a golden streak across a major third. On they soar together, briefly intertwined, then separating as the golden streak chases its silver companion in a steep descent through a spectrum of colors, almost too red for the eye to see, too beautiful for the soul to bear. Now they are on one level again, though separated, swooping in graceful arcs from pine tree to pine tree, spinning gossamer bridges of parallel quints. At last in matched vibrato they turn upward together, ascending in a soaring, exulting climax, their path creating a flame as they approach the crest.

There they remain suspended for an instant, then turn earthward with infinite grace, as exultation slowly ebbs to a whisper. The flame burns blue now in its last flicker, growing smaller, smaller, smaller, almost extinct, engulfed in the mighty stillness of the forest.

Deeply moved by this marriage of sound and sight, you sit down to meditate. And as you meditate, you feel new combinations, new creative possibilities slowly coming to life within you, growing, expanding, clamoring for expression. Watch them grow, let them take shape, until you can express them smoothly, effortlessly, confidently.

The Flame of Spirit Itself

I can identify myself heartily with nothing in me except with the flame of spirit itself. Therefore the truest picture of my inmost being would show none of the features of my person, and nothing of the background of my life. It would show only the light of understanding that burned within me and, as far as it could, consumed and purified all the rest.

George Santayana

Greater Creative Powers

Here is a tradition that darkly counterpoints the political and economic history of man: a deep and indispensable soil of psychic shape-shifting from which a wealth of human self-knowledge grows. It has been, invariably, in moments of trance or dizzy transport that men and women have approached nearest the gods and been inspired (breathed into) by creative powers greater than their normal own.

Theodore Roszak

We Begin Our "Going Down"

We spend most of our time and energy in a kind of horizontal thinking. We move along the surface of things going from one quick base to another, often with a frenzy that wears us out. We collect data, things, people, ideas, "profound experiences," never penetrating any of them . . .

But there are other times. There are times when we stop. We sit still. We lose ourselves in a pile of leaves or its memory. We listen and breezes from a whole other world begin to whisper. Then we begin our "going down."

James Carroll

171

32.

Moods of Love I

Moods exist in time. If you wish to create a mood, you must create a kind of time environment in which the mood can blossom, regardless of the characteristics of the present moment. This is not time distortion, but manipulation of actual clock time.

One way to manipulate time is to create a story, because story sequences require images, and images are born and sustained in time.

The theme of the following story-vignette is love—an emotion capable of many moods and guises. Your task is to translate the images into a mood, and to make the mood your own.

PREPARATION

GOAL
Evoking and sustaining a mood.

TIME
One hour.

Read the following vignette in your reality state, then put yourself into your altered state of consciousness using one of your favorite relaxation techniques.

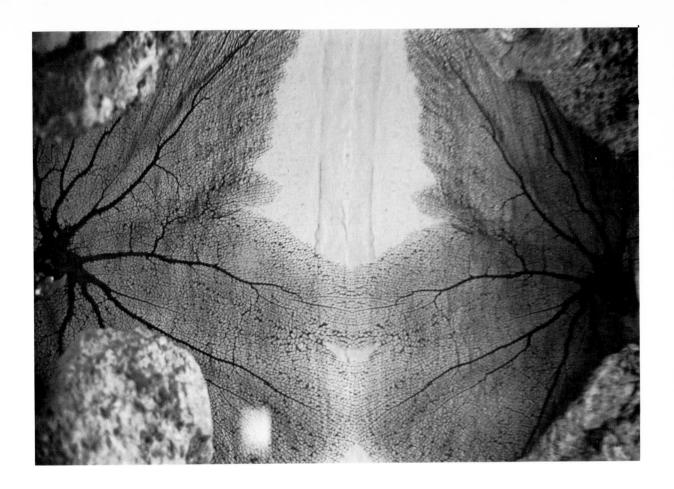

THE VIGNETTE

A young man is striding along a snow-covered mountain path, surrounded by the stillness of a luminous winter night. Only the crunching of snow beneath his feet breaks the quiet. Above him the sky stretches endlessly in all directions— so star-studded that it seems like an immense umbrella of light sprinkled with bits of darkness. The entire panorama, from the distant peaks and valleys to the trees alongside his path, is bathed in an unearthly light.

He comes upon a clearing, and the source of light is suddenly revealed: Raptly he looks at the full moon which seems to draw him closer as it does all things on earth, but yet has singled him out above all other things.

Exultation

There dawned upon me a new knowledge of what divineness can lodge in a woman's soul . . . the first intoxication of that opening glory, the buoyancy which lifts beyond the clutch of fate, the sheer exultation that in the universe such a creature could breathe and live.

F. W. H. Myers

The Core Experience

To love is to approach each other center to center.

Pierre Teilhard de Chardin

The Renewing Flood

The very heavens seemed to open and pour down rays of light and glory. Not for a moment only, but all day and night, floods of light and glory seemed to pour through my soul, and oh, how I was changed, and everything became new. My horses and hogs and everybody seemed changed.

From a case quoted by William James

This is not the barren moon of science, invaded and explored by missiles, nor the romantic symbol of a thousand popular songs. This is the moon of Oscar Wilde's *Salome*—a beautiful woman, a princess with snow-white doves as feet. His eyes are riveted upon her. Her glow lights his face.

He feels motion in his motionless legs, feels himself moving toward her, wanting, willing her to meet him. His every sense is keyed to peak awareness, yet he is oblivious of the icy coldness of the wind and the stinging slap of snow from the wind-bent branches.

He feels the pale moon-woman's floating motion toward him as much as his purposeful advance toward her. They are drawn to each other as if magnetized. Now they are close. He opens his arms and embraces the shadowy form, which takes on substance from contact with him. Their shapes blend together.

The merging of their outlines extends to their minds and pervades their blood. He experiences their unity with every fiber; every muscle and sinew in him responds, grows strong in ways they had not been strong before. The wind has joined their union and supports them, carrying them along on violent gusts.

There is a soaring in his mind and heart, almost unbearable in intensity. At last, when the ultimate crescendo has been reached, it begins to abate. The shadow form slips out of the hold of his arms and is borne away by the wind. He is left alone with the purity of night and snow, never to be lonely again, filled with the afterglow of new heights of aliveness.

THE EXERCISE

When you have reached a fairly deep state of mind, recreate the vignette in minute detail, perhaps even substituting yourself for the hero or heroine. As you do this, a mood will be born in you. It will grow in intensity as it becomes reinforced by personal memories or daydreams. Let the mood carry you wherever it leads. Suffuse yourself with the sights, the sounds, and the gestures. *Live* the mood.

At the end, before awakening yourself by the one-to-three count, establish a key symbol for this mood in your inner mind, to help you return to the story environment and to the mood easily on future occasions.

Enveloping Shadows

A black tall slim shadow
against the blue-grey
water coming in small waves
in from faded sky
the shadow flat
not molded round like
sculpture or man
shallow or hollow
as a shadow
or a mirror dark
entrance to another world
where it is the beast
I come but do not fit
the shadow
my yellow hair flies soft
in the bare wind
my shadow white and round
against blue-black water
the shadow shrinks
down to my size moves
as if to embrace me
shrinks more
into my white arms
into my white thighs
into my belly
into my head until
I finally sink
into its dark beast shape
and become one
with its dark world beyond
fill the space and
finally am one with the world.

Anonymous
Four Visions

Passion is Part of Living

In sex it is the attitude of experiencing sexual desire and passion as one aspect of interpersonal relationships. Separating sex from the rest of self, indeed, is no more tenable than to isolate one's larynx and speak of "my vocal cords wanting to talk with my friend."

Rollo May

33.

Moods of Love II

PREPARATION

Read the following vignette in your reality state. Then enter your altered state of consciousness, this time perhaps choosing a different route. (The more trails you blaze to the deeper levels of your mind, the better. On occasion, you may find that one particular passage into the trance state is blocked, while another is perfectly accessible.) Recreate and experience the vignette with all your senses, and before awakening yourself by the one-to-three count, establish a key symbol for easy reentry into the vignette experience in the future.

THE VIGNETTE

It is summer now on the mountain path, and the young man is slowed by the oppressive heat as he walks laboriously, not bothering to glance at the green tops of the trees along the path or the haze-shrouded horizon of mountains and valleys. The air is motionless, betraying no hint of the currents driving the black clouds overhead. The man's bare back glistens with a film of perspiration.

A distant rumble heralds the awakening of a sleeping force. Then all is silence again, but it is a silence that holds its breath. Some of the silent energy enters him, causing a flexing of muscles and emotions.

GOAL
Evoking and sustaining a mood.

TIME
One hour.

Tears

My last hope fell
like some autumn leaf
in the musty rain,
and I could not pray words.

I walked along the sea.

When the sun vanished,
the rain stretched down
to cleanse my face.

My tears opened me,
the way spring blooms roses.

Alice Sullivan

The Peak Experience

I walked through mists and clouds, breathing the thin air of high altitudes and stepping on slippery ice and snow, till at last through a gateway of clouds, as it seemed, to the very paths of the sun and moon, I reached the summit, completely out of breath and nearly frozen to death.

Basho

A second rumble, closer and louder. A flash of lightning streaks across his line of vision. The energy inside him surges, gathering itself for an explosive outpouring. He is filled with expectancy, a knowledge of the inevitability of the approaching thunderous climax.

The next stab of light seems to pierce his marrow. His lips form a shout, but his voice is drowned in the shattering crash of thunder. For a moment he knows extinction, within him and around him. Then the rains come—a drop, a trickle, a stream, a flood, a torrent—drenching, inundating the parched earth as if land were turning into sea. He feels the rain on his face, his arms, his shoulders and back. He stands and lets the water beat upon him. He welcomes it.

Then, as abruptly as it came, the rain ceases, as though it had never been; and yet all is different —the earth is depleted as well as renewed.

He closes his eyes, and on his lids feels the caress of the returning sun. His body is bathed in warmth and light, untouched by the vapor rising from the earth around him. He is at peace, invigorated as after many hours' sleep, transformed by a dream he knows was not a dream but a new kind of reality, a reality he had not known before.

Union

The life instinct, or sexual instinct, demands activity of a kind that, in contrast to our current mode of activity, can only be called play. The life instinct also demands a union with others and with the world around us based not on anxiety and aggression but on narcissism and erotic exuberance.

Norman O. Brown

Beams of Love

And we are put on earth a little space,
That we may learn to bear the beams of love.

William Blake

34.
Transition

PREPARATION

Put yourself into your trance state by either a relaxation, or eye-fixation method.

When you have reached your altered state of consciousness, tell yourself that you will count from ten to zero, and on reaching zero will have regressed in time to your adolescence. Do not suggest a specific age, but ask your subconscious to focus on the period when you most acutely felt the emotional and physical pangs of growing up. Give your inner mind a few moments to comply, then ask it to name the specific age. The first figure that comes to your mind will be the correct one.

GOAL
To heighten self-understanding by reliving the process of growth and development, in harmony with the movements of the seasons.

TIME
About 30 minutes.

THE EXERCISE

Now that you are an adolescent again, think of yourself in analogy to spring; feel the special poignancy of this transitional state, the sense of greenness, freshness, curiosity—youth in its inevitable movement toward summer.

With every passing moment your sense of identity with the most exciting of the seasons becomes more acute. You can feel spring in you: One moment you are swept by a chilly wind, and black clouds fill your horizon; rain pelts and batters everything in its path. An instant later, the clouds disperse and sunshine floods your private universe.

Born Free

Compulsion is being trapped in a known psychic reality, a dead-end space. Freedom is in the unknown. If you believe there is an unknown everywhere, in your own body, in your relationships with other people, in political institutions, in the universe, then you have maximum freedom. If you can examine old beliefs and realize they are limits to be overcome and can also realize you don't have to have a belief about something you don't yet know anything about, you are free.

John C. Lilly

Escape From Emptiness

The present moment is significant, not as the bridge between past and future, but by reason of its contents, contents which can fill our emptiness and become ours, if we are capable of receiving them.

Dag Hammarskjöld

Reaching Upward

Like a young plant hitherto quietly and intermittently developing which suddenly begins to breathe harder and to grow, as though in a miraculous hour it has become aware of the law which shapes it and begins to strive toward the fulfillment of its being, the boy, touched by the magician's hand, began rapidly and eagerly to gather and tauten his energies. He felt changed, growing; he felt new tensions and new harmonies between himself and the world. There were times, now, in music, Latin, and mathematics, when he could master tasks that were still far beyond his age and the scope of his schoolmates. Sometimes he felt capable of any achievements. At other times he might forget everything and daydream with a new softness and surrender, listen to the wind or the rain, gaze into the chalice of a flower or the moving waters of the river, understanding nothing, divining everything, lost in sympathy, curiosity, the craving to comprehend, carried away from his own self toward another, toward the world, toward the mystery and sacrament, the at once painful and lovely disporting of the world of appearances.

Hermann Hesse

But while the clouds are in the ascendant, they infect you with their contagious blackness, and you, in turn, affect your surroundings. Inevitably, your family participates in your upheaval. You are as exasperated with yourself as they are.

Your awkward body defies you as you defy them; your voice refuses to accept your control, as you refuse to accept theirs; most of all your mind is in your way—your volatile, churning mind, the focal point of all your miseries. You look at yourself in the mirror, and see a stranger who seems to be wearing your face by mistake. From your features, the sense of unreality spreads to the rest of your body and to the actuality which surrounds you: Is that really *you* standing before your mirror in your room, and is that room really *your* room?

Now pause a moment, and consciously relax every muscle of this up-tight adolescent. Feel all the awkwardness drain out, and when you are quite drained of it, summon the future which you already know: your mature body which knows how to work and to play, your responsive mind which has learned to focus and concentrate, your spirit which unifies and integrates everything you do. It is the summer of your lifetime, just around the corner.

Then begin the ascent into the future which is your present age; and feel, together with your own growth, your own progress, the unity of all generations and of all living things in nature.

Growth to Wholeness

Chaos is the path to a greater wholeness of being and consciousness: a path, a transition, a process. The Sage is he who, first of all, understands this process, feels its rhythm, realizes the meaning of its polar attractions and repulsions. He is the man who sees all nature as a cyclic interplay of energies between "lesser wholes" and "greater wholes." Within him as without, he witnesses individual pain transforming itself into collective peace, and collective fulfillment sacrificing itself into the inspiration and guidance which those who are identified with the "greater whole" can bestow upon "lesser wholes" still struggling with the problems of their atomistic and painful relationships.

Dane Rudhyar

The Self in Past and Future

Psyche is transition, hence necessarily to be defined under two aspects. On the one hand, the psyche gives a picture of the remnants and traces of the entire past, and, on the other, but expressed in the same picture, the outlines of the future, inasmuch as the psyche creates its own future.

C. G. Jung

35.
Echoes From the Future

INTRODUCTORY NOTE

You are in the summer of your lifetime—or perhaps only in the spring. With this comforting knowledge to fall back on, prepare now for a glimpse of your autumn years by means of hypnotic progression.

PREPARATION

In an earlier exercise you experienced age regression in an altered state; you returned to an earlier age—not by remembering, but in an experience of acute reliving. Your movements, thoughts, and even your handwriting were again what they actually were in your childhood. The present altered state exercise involves *progression* in time. Age progression in an altered state could be called a special form of ESP: your body and mind not only foresee, but actually pre-experience the you of a future age on a physiological, mental, and emotional plane.

The possibility of pre-experiencing old age has been validated by research. Experimental subjects in their twenties were given objective tests both in the waking state and under the hypnotically-induced belief that they were 65 years

GOAL
To pre-experience old age, accompanied by a realization of the latent potential within you, and a growth in your empathy with older people. You may find that one of the many things your deeper mind can do is to bridge the generation gap.

TIME
30 to 45 minutes.

old. Responses of the young people pre-experiencing old age closely paralleled the actual responses made by people in the 60-65-year group.

In this exercise, your task will be to transport yourself to an age considerably older than your current one, and in the trance state to produce your own future reactions to present stimuli.

In the waking state, study and reflect on these facts: The waking responses of a 22-year-old experimental subject when compared to responses made during hynoptic progression to age 65 reveal some strong differences. With age, we forget how to remember facts and details; we lack the speed and flexibility in decision-making that we had at a younger age; we find abstract reasoning more difficult—it's harder as we grow older to see the relationship between a poem and a statue. The most dramatic change, however, occurs in the area of emotions.

Slow Pace

To climb steep hills requires slow pace at first.

William Shakespeare

Getting There Ahead of Time

I am talking about the possibility of choosing **or** creating **our own styles of development in later life. Much of what gives old age its special character has to do with the state of one's mind and one's interpersonal relationships.**

Suppose that a person could pre-experience **himself as old while he was still chronologically young. What an opportunity this would be to develop strategies and resources for actual old age.**

Robert Kastenbaum

For example, in a young woman taking a word association test the stimulus word "sixteen" elicited the response "age"; the same woman, hypnotically experiencing old age, responded with the word "number." To the stimulus word "fellow" this young girl gave the warm, personal response "friend"; as an old woman, her response became the impersonal "boy."

In the waking state, the young woman had no fear responses to the thoughts of being lost or in pain; yet both these thoughts stimulated strong fear responses while she was hypnotically pre-experiencing herself at the age of 65.

Now, sitting in a comfortable armchair or lying in bed, relax and close your eyes. Put yourself in your altered state of consciousness.

THE EXERCISE

See yourself in a familiar room, facing its door from the opposite wall. Now that you reflect on it, this familiar room has two unfamiliar aspects: The door seems larger than you remember it, and the floor between you and the door tilts slightly upward.

You decide to explore and cross the room, feeling the strain of the incline in your legs. You open the door, and are confronted with another room and another door—this one still larger, and the tilt of the floor more pronounced. You cross that room and open the new door, and beyond it is a third door, across an even steeper floor, and each succeeding door is larger, each floor steeper. . . . You are really climbing a mountain, higher and higher, steeper and steeper, until at last you reach the summit and see the new panorama.

The you that now stands on the mountain top is not the same you that began the climb. The path from the familiar room to the unknown summit covers not only distance but also time. Each upward step was a step into future time, and the doors were the aggregate of years, each larger than the last. You are now thirty years older than you were when you started out.

And now you proceed to explore this newly-old you. Concentrate your thoughts on a field of interest, an activity, or a personal concern which occupies much of your waking thoughts in your normal consciousness, and in which you are emotionally involved. Focus on several possible outcomes of this dominant concern, making them as specific as possible. Silently verbalize and mentally record your first, instinctive response to each.

Don't rush, and stay very, very relaxed . . . very much at ease. If your concentration tends to lighten your trance, deepen it again by a slow ten-to-zero count, then return to focusing on your responses, without urgency or stress, as if you were concentrating pleasurably on a fascinating game.

Do this for as long as you feel so inclined, as long as instinctive responses come to your mind. When you feel yourself running dry, prepare for the wake-up count, suggesting that it will insure a prompt return to your real age in the present time. But before you count from one to three and open your eyes, suggest to yourself that you will remember each of your pre-experienced responses, so that you can check them against your reactions in the waking state and, if you wish, against the waking responses of older people you know.

A New Frontier

I saw that if I could go 50 years ahead, everybody would leave me alone. And that's exactly the way it happened. I was allowed to do anything I wanted and people said, "Well, you're very amusing, but obviously I can't take you seriously." But because I'd deliberately got to living and thinking 50 years ahead on a comprehensive basis, I inadvertently got myself into a strange position. I began to live on that frontier, and it was like any wave phenomenon: I was living where it was cresting and things happened to me long before they happened to the rest of society.

R. Buckminster Fuller

A Second Chance

In our studies, my colleagues and I try to establish a situation that resembles the one in which an old person is likely to find himself. We then challenge the young or middle-aged adult to function under the handicaps or rules that the aged most often encounter. Unlike the old person, however, this participant gets a second chance—or as many second chances as he would like—to develop a strategy for mastering the situation.
Robert Kastenbaum

36.
Perchance to Dream

INTRODUCTORY NOTE

With this exercise we move into a new area and, once again, you must practice scales before you can play a sonata: Gradually, your unconscious will acquire the habit of responding to your needs in the dream state; after some practice you will learn to remember and to utilize the material of your dreams.

PREPARATION

This exercise is best practiced at night, before going to sleep. Place a note pad and pencil within easy reach near your bed, settle down comfortably, and turn off the light. With your eyes closed, induce an altered state of consciousness by means of a relaxation technique.

THE EXERCISE

When you feel yourself to be in a light to medium trance, tell yourself that you will shortly drop off to sleep, and that you will, upon awakening, have a clear recollection of one of your dreams. (Usually people have more than one dream each night.) Repeat this suggestion two or three times slowly and emphatically, without, however, suggesting any guidelines as to dream content. Then allow yourself to drift off.

GOAL
To tap the powers of the unconscious mind in the dream state, for enhanced creativity or solving specific problems.

TIME
Approximately ten minutes per session.

You will either awaken in the middle of the night with a clear memory of a dream, or you will remember it on awakening in the morning. In either case, be sure to jot down on your note pad key words concerning the dream's content, since you will probably have no time or inclination to record it in full at this time. These notations, however, will bring back the dream in its entirety when you are ready to write it down.

Darkness and Light

We have to surpass the Enlightenment notion that in the life of the species or of the individual there is a definitive change-over from darkness to light. Light is always light in darkness; that is what the unconscious is all about. Nor can the light become a current, always turned on, in ordinary prosaic language. Truth is always in poetic form; not literal but symbolic; hiding, or veiled; light in darkness. Yes, mysterious. Literalism is idolatry of words; the alternative to idolatry is mystery.

Norman O. Brown

Going East

I was skimming along over hill and dale, particularly over snowy hill-tops, and flying with me were three birds of an unearthly blue. Suddenly I exclaimed to anyone who might be listening, "Why, we're going East!" One of the birds looked up rather saucily at me, and all at once the birds were cardinals of as bright a red as they had been a bright blue.

Dream of a College Girl

Symbols

The unconscious activity of modern man ceaselessly presents him with innumerable symbols, and each of them has a particular message to transmit, a particular mission to accomplish, in order to ensure or to re-establish the equilibrium of the psyche. As we have seen, the symbol not only makes the world "open" but also helps religious man to attain to the universal. For it is through symbols that man finds his way out of his particular situation and "opens himself" to the general and the universal. Symbols awaken individual experience and transmute it into a spiritual act, into metaphysical comprehension of the world.

Mircea Eliade

After repeating this procedure on two or three successive nights, set yourself a more difficult task by suggesting that you will recall more than one dream this night. Suggest also that you will awaken several times during the night, each time with a fresh dream recollection, which should always be recorded in key words for subsequent elaboration.

Once you have acquired some facility at this task, you are ready for creative dream utilization.

Perhaps you have a personal problem—it may be an important decision or an interpersonal difficulty or the need for a creative insight—which has defied solution at the waking level. Put yourself into your altered state of consciousness as described above; but this time suggest to yourself that you will dream a dream which will either provide, or point to, a solution of your problem.

Then tell yourself that you will now recapitulate the problem, but without any tension, worry, or fear. You will remain relaxed and serene, insulated by your protective shield of altered consciousness. In that relaxed state, trace the problem in as much detail as possible, both verbally and visually—as if you were telling yourself a story, accompanied by many illustrations. When you have finished, tell yourself once more that you will now go to sleep, and have a dream which will provide, or point the way to, the story's happy ending.

The dream you will dream may take a completely unexpected form. Approach its interpretation without preconceived notions; your subconscious is under no obligation to produce a solution which your conscious mind may have vaguely envisaged. On the contrary, because your subconscious is creative and unfettered by reality orientation, it is more likely to shun the obvious. If the dream content is not immediately clear to you, if it seems ambiguous, keep thinking about it in a relaxed, confident state. The true meaning will emerge, and when it does, you will recognize it instantly by the profound sense of certainty you will experience.

Another Sleep

During sleep, we cross the threshold of a new existence—we are receptive to subliminal and telepathic thoughts. During the waking state, we concentrate on events and sensations in our conscious environment and, in a sense, defend ourselves from sensory perceptions on other levels of awareness. This defensiveness, however, loses some of its intensity when we withdraw from the conscious plane. It is as if we become distant, disembodied observers of ourselves, wandering in a strange world, detached from everyday life. In the dream state, for example, there is no longer any sensation of weight; and we often live in the past or the future . . .

Allan Angoff

A Different Truth

Dreams have a poetic integrity and truth. This limbo and dust-hole of thought is presided over by a certain reason, too. Their extravagance from nature is yet within a higher nature. They seem to us to suggest an abundance and fluency of thought not familiar to the waking experience. They pique us by independence of us, yet we know ourselves in this mad crowd, and owe to dreams a kind of divination and wisdom. My dreams are not me; they are not Nature, or the Not-me; they are both. They have a double consciousness, at once subjective and objective.

Ralph Waldo Emerson

NOTE

If after much reflection, the meaning of the dream is still not clear, repeat the exercise, recapitulating the entire problem while in an altered state, then suggesting sleep and a dream that will help solve the problem. If the same dream occurs the second night, this indicates that the subconscious is very definite about its solution to the problem. However, the subconscious may provide an alternate dream to support, modify or clarify the earlier one. Again, think about the dreams in a relaxed state, confident that the meaning will emerge.

Dreams Awake

Our truest life is when we are in dreams awake.

Henry David Thoreau

Unopened Letter

A dream which is not understood is like a letter which is not opened.

Talmud

37.
Free Fall

GOAL

You may want to try such an act of creation, using your altered state of consciousness in the form of a trance-induced dream.

Perhaps, your fictional character is a seemingly cut-and-dried executive type—successful, financially comfortable. Nothing sets him apart from thousands of his kind. And yet something *is* different: His relaxed manner does not ring quite true to you; there is a muted quality to his gayest moods; even when he is the life of the party, there is a veil of privacy and remoteness in his eyes. Although you have created him, his personality seems to escape even you, retreating into a mysterious dimension from which you are excluded. The mystery keeps nagging at you, because while it persists he is not fully your creation—a flaw in the fabric of your story. There is a way of solving the dilemma: let a dream invent his past. The following exercise presents a sample of such a dream solution.

INTRODUCTORY NOTE

You need not have a problem in order to be helped and enriched by your dreams; your whole life can be immeasurably enhanced by making creative use of them. By means of them you can travel to new countries, new continents, new galaxies; you can return to the past and you can explore the future. You can even invent lives— and live them.

This isn't as far-fetched as it seems. Writers of fiction do it all the time; and if you have tried your hand at writing a novel or short story, you know that developing a character is a complex art. Because real men and women are composites of all that has happened to them since birth, the fictional creation of lifelike people requires that their creator know them not only in the context of the here-and-now of which he writes, but also in the context of all the experiences that went into the shaping of their present selves. He must, in short, endow them with a complete lifetime, even if he only uses a segment of it in his writing.

PREPARATION

Before going to sleep, put yourself into your altered consciousness, and see your character as the adult he is now, clearly and in great detail. Tell yourself that you will shortly go to sleep, and will have a dream which will answer your questions. Formulate them explicitly: Why do his eyes seem to hold memories of pain? Was his success too dearly bought? What was the price he had to pay?

THE EXERCISE

Now you feel yourself slipping into reverie, and from there into dream, accompanied by his figure, which grows younger and younger, as you dream back to his twenties, his adolescence, his childhood.

THE DREAM

Even in the dream you feel the shock wave of surprise:

The child sits in a wheelchair, his motionless legs in braces. His breathing is labored. The noises of a crowded neighborhood reach him through the street-level window, reverberating in the small room, grating on his ears. A victim of polio, he tries hard to count his blessings. Even sitting motionless in the depressing room is much, much better than the prison of the iron lung where he was confined for months. But the road back to health stretches interminably and terrifyingly before him. He looks down at his steel-encased legs. How will he teach them to walk again? When will he get out of this chair, this room, this house, this neighborhood?

He grits his teeth—something he has done so often lately that his jawline is beginning to reflect it. A resolve which has almost hardened into second nature is rekindled. He no longer asks himself whether he can make it; he knows he must, because he cannot accept a half-life, he cannot remain a prisoner of his body.

Someday he will breathe normally again—or, if not quite normally, then only he will know and feel the hardship. And he will walk again, on straight legs, without cane and without limp, no matter what it may cost in time and pain, in isolation and loneliness.

And he does accomplish all of this, in year after year of bitter determination.

A successful executive, he now breathes without apparent effort, and walks with a brisk step younger than his years. He has left behind the street-floor apartment for a home in the suburbs, insulated from street noises. There is no wheelchair, no iron lung, no cane, no limp. There are only his eyes to betray him.

One Important Fact

My mind-body left to itself will unerringly select the one important fact that must be emphasized. . . .

Jeannette Lee

The Universe of Dreams

The Senoi believes that any human being, with the aid of his fellows, can outface, master, and actually utilize all beings and forces in the dream universe. His experience leads him to believe that, if you cooperate with your fellows or oppose them with good will in the day time, their images will eventually help you in your dreams, and that every person should and can become the supreme ruler and master of his own dream or spiritual universe, and can demand and receive help and cooperation of all the forces there.

Kilton Stewart

Self-communication

Both dreams and myths are important communications from ourselves to ourselves. If we do not understand the language in which they are written, we miss a great deal of what we know and tell ourselves in those hours when we are not busy manipulating the outside world.

Erich Fromm

38.
Whirlpool

INTRODUCTORY NOTE

GOAL
To enhance the quality of thinking, in order to clarify one's views on abstract, spiritual, or transcendental matters.

TIME
Approximately one hour.

As the human embryo retraces the physical evolution of the species, so each of us, to reach spiritual maturity, must build on man's heritage. Each of us is faced with personal challenges to evolve religious beliefs, to formulate concepts of the universe, and to understand our purpose on the planet earth at this point in history.

One particular state of consciousness may facilitate the process of reflecting on these challenges. Aldous Huxley discovered the existence of this state within himself, and named it "Deep Reflection." Akin to but not identical with hypnosis, it involves utter relaxation and profound withdrawal from external stimuli, followed by total immersion in the question or problem of interest. Huxley used it for creative purposes in connection with his work.

In the following exercise, guidelines are given for achieving this state of mind.

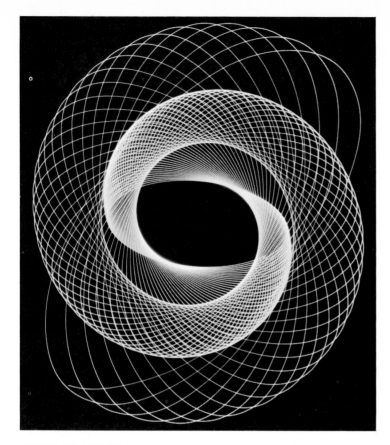

PREPARATION

Sit in a comfortable chair and close your eyes. Imagine yourself sitting on a riverbank, observing the configurations of a whirlpool directly in front of you. A small branch drifts toward the eddy, comes closer and closer, and is finally caught by its pull. Your mind's eye now has a focal point, and follows the progress of the branch caught in the vortex of swirling water, drawing a circle around its largest circumference, then around the next one and the one after that, being drawn down deeper and deeper, faster and faster.

Retaining your sense of comfort and safety, you begin to identify with the branch. Feeling no fear or threat, you follow the branch, you *are* the branch, letting go, relaxing as the whirlpool carries you into its center. You feel relief that the burden of voluntary control is lifted from you, relief at being allowed to let go, to follow where the water leads, deeper and deeper, into a mysterious depth, leading to the new dimension beneath the point of the funnel.

The Unseen Potential

The creative element in the mind of man, that latency which can conceive gods, carve statues, move the heart within the symbols of great poetry, or devise formulas of modern physics, emerges in as mysterious a fashion as those elementary particles which leap into momentary existence in great cyclotrons, only to vanish again like infinitesimal ghosts. The reality we know in our limited lifetimes is dwarfed by the unseen potential of the abyss where science stops. In a similar way the smaller universe of the individual brain has its lonely cometary passages, or flares suddenly like a super nova, only to subside in death while the waves of energy it has released roll on through unnumbered generations.

Loren Eiseley

An Activity of Intuition

It will come about as the result of biochemical discoveries that will make it possible for large numbers of men and women to achieve a radical self-transcendence and a deeper understanding of the nature of things. And this revival of religion will be at the same time a revolution. From being an activity mainly concerned with symbols, religion will be transformed into an activity concerned mainly with experience and intuition—an everyday mysticism underlying and giving significance to everyday rationality, everyday tasks and duties, everyday human relationships.

Aldous Huxley

THE EXERCISE

You have reached your altered state of consciousness by a new route. Now tell yourself that the terminal point of this route, the place where you now find yourself, will be a permanently available starting point for spiritual adventures of your mind; and that from now on you will reach it easily whenever you so desire, by choosing the route of the whirlpool. This route will always lead to the place where you now are—the land of deep reflection.

Now that you have reached this quiet place and identified it, you begin to explore it. There are some landmarks here, which in the future will immediately reinforce your knowledge of having arrived. Take note of them. These landmarks generate in you a new sense of relaxed waiting. Notice how it feels. You will want to remember and recognize it. It is a state too serene to be called expectancy, for you are waiting for something as yet undefined, and yet you know beyond doubt that it will come in good time. The feeling is one of waiting, waiting not for a concrete solution to a concrete problem, but for a panorama of creative thought.

While you are waiting, calmly empty your mind of all other concerns—as if you were clearing a table to spread out on it the pieces of a picture puzzle. There must be plenty of room to display all the pieces of your reflective thoughts. Each piece must lie within its own island of space, so

The Descent into Self

And so, for the first time in my life perhaps, I took the lamp and, leaving the zone of everyday occupations and relationships where everything seems clear, I went down into my inmost self, to the deep abyss whence I feel dimly that my power of action emanates. But as I moved further and further away from the conventional certainties by which social life is superficially illuminated, I became aware that I was losing contact with myself. At each step of the descent a new person was disclosed within me of whose name I was no longer sure, and who no longer obeyed me. And when I had to stop my exploration because the path faded from beneath my steps, I found a bottomless abyss at my feet, and out of it comes—arising I know not from where—the current which I dare to call MY life.

Pierre Teilhard de Chardin

These Unknown Forces

I do not believe that inspiration falls from heaven. I think it rather the result of a profound indolence and of our incapacity to put to work certain forces in ourselves. These unknown forces work deep within us, with the aid of the elements of daily life, its scenes and passions, and, when they burden us and oblige us to conquer the kind of somnolence in which we indulge ourselves like invalids who try to prolong dream and dread resuming contact with reality, in short when the work that makes itself in us and in spite of us demands to be born, we can believe that this work comes to us from beyond and is offered us by the gods.

Jean Cocteau

that you can examine it from all angles and study its color and shape for clues. And there must also be enough room for the elements of the solution to join eventually, at first with one complement and then with another, and each of those with *their* complements, until at last all the pieces have found their natural, form-determined partners, and now coalesce into one, incredibly intricate and yet divinely simple, meaningful whole.

Like picture puzzles, reflective problems are often too intricate to be completed in one session. If yours is of this kind, be satisfied with whatever partial meaning has emerged through the joining of scattered pairs, trios, or quartets. There is no need to destroy those configurations by sweeping all the pieces off the table; leave your puzzle spread out, and tell yourself that you will find it exactly as you left it, when you next return to take up your reflective task.

Now prepare to return to your reality state by emerging from the whirlpool: Tell yourself that you will, in a moment, count very slowly from one to three and then open your eyes. At the count of one, you will be at the bottom of the whirlpool, at the point of the funnel. In your mind's eye, see yourself pushing off from the bottom; at the count of two, you will have reached the midpoint of the vortex; at three, you will have reached the surface and be free of the whirlpool's pull.

As soon as you open your eyes you will be back in your reality state, feeling very relaxed and at ease, and in excellent health.

The Center of the Self

When real silence is dared, we can come very close to ourselves and to the deep center of the world. "Nothing much happens"; what little happens comes close to everything. When it is allowed to become itself, silence has a power and momentum of its own that can be startling. Vertical thinking and being replace the horizontal busy-ness of daily life. When we dare to stop talking, silence speaks . . .

Silence issues in a word in the way that primordial being issues in expressive being, in the way that God the Father issues in the Son. When a vast stillness had settled over the whole world, the eternal word leapt down. The mystery repeats itself whenever we fall silent.

James Carroll

Nourishing Images

Images of any kind may be compared to physical food. When images add something or direct our energy to higher levels, they nourish us. Poisonous images are those that lead us into useless or frustrating stimulations or misinform or otherwise degrade us. Nourishing images are food of a special sort for something else in us. Most of the time we do not know whether a given image is poison or nourishment for this something. In states of heightened perception, viewing images in stillness, sometimes the person can realize which is taking place in him: something fine in him is being destroyed during an encounter with a photograph, or something coarse in him is being made finer. The wisdom of the psyche is able to distinguish.

Minor White

199

39.

Twilight

GOAL
To enhance the faculty of creativity.

TIME
Usually about five minutes.

INTRODUCTORY NOTE

There is a type of trance which you have known all your life, without being aware of it: the hypnagogic state, also known as reverie. This is the no man's land between true wakefulness and the oblivion of sleep—the period when thoughts are no longer subject to daytime logic, nor yet completely dreamlike.

Largely ignored until recently—except by outstanding minds who have long used it instinctively—the hypnagogic state is now being scientifically investigated, and the results indicate that it is potentially quite as productive as the dream state, and more accessible. Its greatest usefulness lies in liberating the flow of ideas.

PREPARATION

In a very real sense, the mastery of altered states which you have acquired through the preceding exercises constitutes the preparation for the present one: laboratory research reveals a close psychophysiological link — similarity of brain wave patterns—between the altered state of consciousness and the hypnagogic state. Your main task here is consciously to harness a hitherto unconscious activity.

THE EXERCISE

When you have settled down for the night, turn off the light, close your eyes and relax your entire body. Count slowly from ten to zero. Even without giving yourself a specific suggestion, this will result in some degree of altered consciousness, for your mind is by now conditioned to respond to this familiar stimulus.

When you have achieved a light trance, suggest to yourself that during the next few minutes, just before falling asleep, you will become consciously aware of the images and thought fragments that normally fill your mind during the deepening drowsiness; and that you will remember some of them clearly on awakening in the morning. Then allow yourself to drift off, as easily and naturally as you always do.

Repeat this process on several successive nights, each time suggesting more extensive recall of your mental activity and emotional state during the zone between waking and sleeping.

When you have reached some proficiency in this first stage, suggest to yourself that you will, from now on, be fully conscious of your mental ac-

Integrating the Self

Study of Senoi society seems to indicate that they have arrived at this high state of social and physical cooperation and integration through the system of psychology which they have discovered, invented and developed, and that the principles of this system of psychology are understandable in terms of Western scientific thinking . . .

Senoi psychology falls into two categories. The first deals with dream interpretation; the second with dream expression in the agreement trance or cooperative reverie. The cooperative reverie is not participated in until adolescence and serves to initiate the child into the status of adulthood. After adolescence, if he spends a great deal of time in the trance state, a Senoi is considered a specialist in healing or in the use of extra-sensory powers.

Kilton Stewart

202

tivity in this twilight state *even while it is going on:* that your conscious mind will be observing the reverie productions of your semiconscious mind.

During this period you may make some fascinating discoveries about yourself, for the language of reverie, like that of dreams, is symbolic. But because in reverie you are closer to your reasoning self than you are in dreams, the symbols are likely to be clearer, and may reveal many of your unconscious processes to your observing self.

Once you have mastered this second stage, you are ready to put the hypnagogic state to work for you. The next time you feel in the mood for a new project, induce a trance by any relaxation method. Then suggest to yourself that, from now on, you will utilize the hypnagogic period as a creative, self-exploratory technique; that you will now be able to use this state as productively as many outstanding people have used it, including the poets Robert Louis Stevenson and A. E. Houseman, and the physicist Kekulé (whose theory of molecular constitution was formulated in the hypnagogic state). You will be able to control the direction and content of your hypnagogic images. And because their hallmark is creativity, they will deal in a uniquely creative manner with whatever subject—philosophical, metaphysical, artistic, or scientific—occupies your attention.

NOTE

Reinforce this *general suggestion* several times, at intervals of a few days. And the next time you have a *specific subject* in mind, verbalize it in a detailed suggestion in an altered state while lying in bed, preparatory to going to sleep. Then relax, and let your twilight zone take over.

Visions

These are times when the unknown reveals itself to the spirit of man in visions . . . Those that depart still remain near us—they are in a world of light; but they as tender witnesses hover about our world of darkness. Though invisible to some they are not absent. Sweet is their presence; holy is their converse with us.

Victor Hugo
Toilers of the Sea

The Union of Realities

The more faithfully you listen
to the voice within you,
the better you will hear
what is sounding outside.
And only he who listens can speak.
Is this the starting point of the road
towards the union
of your two dreams—
to be allowed in clarity of mind
to mirror life
and in purity of heart to mold it?

Dag Hammerskjöld

Floating

These are our first real experiences of life—floating in a warm fluid, curling inside a total embrace, swaying to the undulations of the moving body, and hearing the beat of the pulsing heart. Our prolonged exposure to these sensations, in the absence of other competing stimuli, leaves a lasting impression on our brains, an impression that spells security, comfort, and passivity.

Desmond Morris

203

40.

Rebirth

INTRODUCTORY NOTE

Certain techniques used in prayer, for example the techniques of Zen meditation, are designed to enable people to pray in an altered state of consciousness. In such a state, prayer reaches a much deeper level than the 'talking to God' style of praying. In the expanded awareness of altered states of consciousness, prayer becomes an experience of the whole person. It does not feed on ideas, but on the lived experience of God which often needs no words. The altered state of consciousness can greatly assist the quiet, contemplative style of prayer in which those who pray are lifted out of themselves and absorbed in the subject they are contemplating.

PREPARATION

In prayer experience, two people are involved—the one who prays and God. In this relationship there is no formula that can provoke an automatic response from God. No one can force a mystical experience, and this is not the object of the exercises. But what is certain is that an altered state of consciousness can lead you to a deeper appreciation of what prayer is and can broaden your prayer experience.

The following two exercises take as themes for prayer two notions fundamental to the religious awareness of mankind—rebirth and our oneness in God with all creation.

GOAL
As has been stated, the goal of this and of the following exercise is simply to enter into the prayer experience on a particular theme.

TIME
Allow one hour.

Rebirth is obviously not a physical reality or a matter of regression into the womb. It is a spiritual experience in which man becomes aware of the creative power of the Spirit within him, re-creating him anew in love. It is an experience of a total acceptance of man by divine love, an acceptance that purifies, enlightens and revivifies man in the inmost depths of his being.

Relax and concentrate your whole self on the thought of the presence of the Spirit of God. Count from ten to zero. As you count, try to become less and less preoccupied with yourself. Tell yourself that when you reach zero you will be filled only with the thought of the presence of the Spirit; all thoughts about yourself will have vanished.

One in Knowledge

The knower and the known are one.
Simple people imagine
that they should see God,
as if He stood there and they here.
This is not so.
God and I, we are one in knowledge.

Meister Eckhart

Cleansing the Heart

Prayer needs no speech. It is in itself independent of any sensuous effort. I have not the slightest doubt that prayer is an unfailing means of cleansing the heart of passions. But it must be combined with the utmost humility.

Gandhi

205

THE EXERCISE

The Spirit of God who fills your consciousness fills the whole earth, the entire cosmos. Let yourself be carried by the Spirit and in him roam over the whole of creation. Feel his power in the mighty winds, his strength in the towering mountains, the thundering cataracts, the vast ocean. The Spirit is power and strength; the Spirit that fills your consciousness.

The Spirit is the warm gentle breeze, the spectrum of the rainbow, the stillness of a star-studded night, the clear trickling mountain rill. The Spirit is the glow of rosy-fingered dawn, the song of the lark. He is the wash of waves on the sandy shore. The Spirit is the clouds that sail lazily over the ocean of the sky. The Spirit is gentleness; the Spirit that fills your consciousness.

The Spirit is the rich fertile earth and the seed in the earth, dying so that it may come to life. He is the myriad, teeming life of ocean and forest. All that lives, lives in him and by him. The tiniest insect that knows but a day's life knows it through him. He is the life of the thousand-year-old sequoia and of the first spring flower. The Spirit gives life to man, a life that changes but never ends. This Spirit is the Spirit of life; the Spirit that fills your consciousness.

The Spirit inspires the hands of the artist who paints in the colors of the Spirit. By the Spirit the sculptor releases from the hard rock the beauty that lies hidden therein. The musician calls forth from his instrument the voice of the Spirit. The Spirit is the Spirit of creativity; the Spirit that fills your consciousness.

The Spirit is the caress of loving hands, the communion of all who love and are loved. He is the bond that binds hearts and minds and bodies in peace and harmony. His dwelling is in love and all that he touches is thereby aglow with love, with warmth, with intimacy. The Spirit is the Spirit of love; the Spirit that fills your consciousness.

To be Slowly Born

No single event can awaken
   within us
a stranger totally unknown to us.
To live is to be slowly born.
It would be a bit too easy
if we could go about borrowing
   ready-made souls.

Antoine De Saint Exupery

Beyond Your Hand

I hold close the womb
where life first lies
between the swinging and the sigh
singing songs to seed within
to seedling yet unborn
who man the states of spaces
   yet unfound
of a universe spinning endless
beyond your hand and mine
turned in the hand of time
I sing of a land of mystery
where the dinosaur came to die
and stamped his print in history
I hold close the womb
where first life lies
and sigh a human sigh
and hope we learn to dance
before we learn to die.

Richard M. Prodey

Together in Yourself

Find your home in the haunts of every living creature. Make yourself higher than all heights and lower than all depths. Bring together in yourself all opposites of quality: heat and cold, dryness and fluidity. Think that you are everywhere at once, on land, at sea, in heaven. Think that you are not yet begotten, that you are in the womb, that you are young, that you are old, that you have died, that you are in the world beyond the grave. Grasp in your thought all this at once, all times and places, all substances and qualities and magnitudes together. Then you can apprehend God.

Hermes Trismegistus

The Procreant Urge of the World

There was never any more inception
  than there is now,
Nor any more youth or age
  than there is now,
And will never be any more perfection
  than there is now,
Nor any more heaven or hell
  than there is now.

Urge and urge and urge,
Always the procreant urge
  of the world.
Out of the dimness opposite equals
  advance, always substance
  and increase, always sex,
Always a knit of identity,
  always distinction,
  always a breed of life.

                  Walt Whitman

In the Purity of Innocence

One has to devote himself with his whole heart and soul to the recovery of his "innocence." And yet, . . . this cannot be the work of our own "self." It is useless for the "self" to "make a place in itself" for God. The innocence and purity of heart which belong to paradise are a complete emptiness of self in which all is the work of God, the free and unpredictable expression of His love, the work of grace. In the purity of original innocence, all is done in us but without us.

                  Thomas Merton

O Hand Unseen

O Hand Unseen, be gentle
  and kind to me,
  Touch me in desperate hour
When I forget thy guidance;
  though I be Impatient
  of thy power,
Yet does my heart elect
To turn along the way
  thou dost direct
To meet the ultimate end,
Content on thee, thee only,
  to depend.

                  Edward Davison

Power, strength, gentleness, life, creativity, love, this is the Spirit that fills you. Give yourself to this Spirit, let his power and strength replace your weakness; his gentleness replace your harshness and your prejudices. Let his life replace all that is dead within you. Let him quicken your dulled perception, your stifled affectivity. Let his love fill you. The Spirit creates, he is creating you anew every moment of your life. In him you are being continually reborn. Go with the Spirit into newness of life.

Give yourself a few moments to emerge slowly from this profound experience. Then tell yourself that you will count from one to three, and open your eyes. As soon as you open them you will be back in your usual reality state, relaxed and at peace.

Show me your original face which you had before your father and mother conceived you! Show me—in other words—your genuine, deepest self, not the self which depends on family and conditioning, on learning or experience, or any kind of artifice.

Alan Watts

41.

Earth, Air, Fire, Water

INTRODUCTORY NOTE

Mechanized, urban living can stifle our awareness of the rhythm of the seasons and of the great cosmic realities of which we are part. By the same token, our religious experience can be stunted and confined to the worship of a city God. This exercise is designed to expand religious awareness by bringing you into contact with the elemental forces of the universe. Through them you will reach out toward the universal God.

PREPARATION

Relax and count slowly from ten to zero. When you have reached your deeper level of mind, allow yourself to be carried to the heart of the great plains at a time before man desecrated their beauty. Stand there for a few moments, barefoot, and feel the vastness of the rolling grasslands. You are alone in a solitude free of loneliness.

GOAL
As in *Rebirth*, to enter into the prayer experience.

TIME
Allow one hour.

THE EXERCISE

Feel the earth beneath your bare feet, dig your toes into the rich, fertile soil. Go deeper: Beneath the soil is bed rock, layer upon ancient layer reaching to the molten center of the world. Go wider: As far as the eye can see there is earth stretching away to the mountains that edge the horizon, and beyond. Turn to the four directions, north, south, east, west. This is the great earth, mother earth from whose womb all life has emerged and still emerges. Lie down and embrace the earth, your earth, the earth from which every life force comes. Feel that life within yourself—a powerful, indestructible force.

The Responsibility of Consciousness

For one who sees the universe in the guise of a laborious communal ascent towards the summit of consciousness, life, far from seeming blind, hard or despicable, becomes charged with gravity, with responsibilities, with new relationships.

Pierre Teilhard de Chardin

Through Consciousness

Through becoming conscious we have been driven out of paradise, through consciousness we can come back to paradise.

Heinrich Jacoby

When You Come to the One

The shell must be cracked apart
if what is in it is to come out,
for if you want the kernel
you must break the shell.
And therefore if you want
to discover nature's nakedness
you must destroy its symbols,
and the farther you get in
the nearer you come to its essence.
When you come to the One
that gathers all things up into itself,
there you must stay.

Meister Eckhart

Now the wind begins to rise, making waves over the grasslands. Rise and face the wind. Let it stream through your hair and feel its coldness on your body. A good coldness, clean and bracing. The wind grows stronger and you bend to meet its gusts. Where does it come from? Where does it go? This air that is the symbol of the Spirit.

Air without which we die, air that feeds every living plant and creature and sculpts even the rocks into strange and beautiful shapes. Air that is the breath of life. Breathe in and out deeply. Your breathing is prayer and communion with the source of life.

Now face the sun where it rises like a ball of fire in the heavens. This sun from whose fiery mass our earth came as an incandescent globe billions of years ago. The sun, source of energy and of life, warming the dead earth of winter into spring's green life. The earth is our mother and the sun our father. Source of light, of fire, of life; source of infinitely expanding radiance. Let the sun's rays bathe your body, let its radiance penetrate deep into your spirit. That radiance is the symbol of the divine power that has brought you into being, that sustains and enlightens your life.

Far off on the horizon clouds begin to rise from behind the mountains. With surprising swiftness they swoop down over the prairie, gradually obscuring the sun. The rain begins to fall, slowly at first, with warm, gentle drops, but quickly becoming a torrent drumming on the surface of the earth. The rain streams down your hair and face and bathes your whole body; water of life, nourishing the seeds and the plant roots deep in the earth. Water without which all that lives would shrivel and wither away. Water of your life.

Earth, air, fire, water—all these elements are life in you and lead you to their source, the source of all life, the divine power that reaches out now to touch you with his life-giving, healing, loving hands.

Drink deep of this experience that needs no words. When you are ready, return to your ordinary consciousness. Count from one to three and open your eyes. You are back in your usual reality state now, but the new dimensions of your spirit remain with you.

To Be and Act and Live

We should understand well that all things are the works of the Great Spirit. We should know that He is within all things: the trees, the grasses, the rivers, the mountains, and all the four-legged animals, and the winged peoples; and even more important, we should understand that He is also above all these things and peoples. When we do understand all this deeply in our hearts, then we will fear, and love, and know the Great Spirit, and then we will be and act and live as He intends.

A prayer of Black Elk

Cosmic Consciousness

The prime characteristic of cosmic consciousness is, as its name implies, a consciousness of the cosmos, that is, of the life and order of the universe. . . . Along with this there occurs an intellectual enlightenment or illumination which alone would place the individual on a new plane of existence—would make him almost a member of a new species. To this is added a state of moral exaltation, an indescribable feeling of elevation, elation, and joyousness, and a quickening of the moral sense, which is fully striking and more important both to the individual and to the race than is the enhanced intellectual power. With these come what may be called a sense of immortality, a consciousness of eternal life, not conviction that he shall have this, but the consciousness that he has it already.

R. M. Bucke

213

42.

Meditation I

INTRODUCTORY NOTE

People are inclined to regard mystical experiences as spontaneous manifestations of a deeply religious spirit. Indeed, many of them are; but the potential range of mystical experiences far exceeds the purely religious realm, and they are often achieved as a result of very specific ascetical training. One such training method is the practice of contemplative meditation, which is the subject of the following two exercises.

Contemplative meditation involves two steps: 1) The active phase of mastering mental concentration; 2) the passive phase of total receptivity. The present exercise deals with Phase I; you yourself will be the best judge as to when you are ready to progress to Phase II.

PREPARATION

GOAL
To reach a higher level of awareness, in which the mind is open to universal, transcendental influences.

TIME
Approximately 30 minutes.

Relax deeply, and go into your altered state of consciousness very gradually, counting from ten to zero. Remain on that plateau for a while, emptying your mind as much as possible of all extraneous thought. Then count from ten down

214

A Steady Aim

Before an instrument can be used it must be created. It is true that most men learn to concentrate on worldly affairs, but all such effort is directed towards the analysis, synthesis and comparison of facts and ideas, while the Concentration which is a necessary prelude to Meditation aims at unwavering focus on the chosen thing or idea to the exclusion of any other subject . . . complete one-pointedness of thought upon the subject in hand, be it a pencil, a virtue, or a diagram imagined in the mind.

Christmas Humphreys

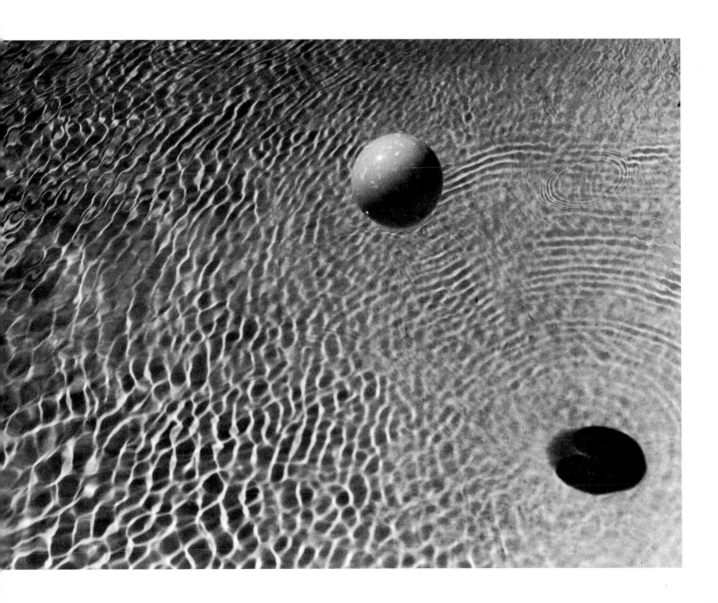

The Gift of Wonder

**The most beautiful experience
we can have is the mysterious.
It is the fundamental emotion
which stands at the cradle
of true art and true science.
Whoever does not know it
and can no longer wonder,
no longer marvel,
is as good as dead,
and his eyes are dimmed.**

Albert Einstein

to zero again, suggesting that this time, on arriving at zero, you will be very deeply in trance, very, very deeply—much deeper than you have ever been before, so deeply as to approach a state of suspended animation. You are quite motionless, everything in you is stilled except your breathing. Suggest to yourself that if, in the course of performing this exercise, your altered state should lighten, you will merely have to draw three deep breaths to return to the deepest level of which you are capable to date.

THE EXERCISE

Now that you have reached this new level of mind, which is deeper than any you have known before, establish before your inner eye the image of a vase, a vase of simple, graceful lines. Trace its outline visually behind your closed lids, circling its rim, following its curved shape downward, down to the delicately balanced base. Now step back, as it were, from this close inspection, and see the vase in its entirety again—and see it *alone,* to the exclusion of everything else.

Let no other objects, nor even vague background blurs, dilute your singleminded concentration on the vase; and do not allow yourself to reflect on it in any way. Your only task is to keep the image of the vase before your inner eye.

The moment you feel your concentration lagging, your attention wandering, recall yourself to the task at hand. If your trance lightens under the effort of focusing, take three deep breaths, without letting the vase out of your sight while reestablishing your trance depth. Then continue in this state of suspended animation, with all your faculties fused into the single task of observing the vase.

When you feel you have reached the limit of your attention span, allow the vase to fade gradually into a neutral background. Then tell yourself that you will now count from one to three and open your eyes. As soon as you have opened them you will be back in your reality state, feeling extremely relaxed, and in perfect health.

Practice this exercise as often as necessary, until you master the art of concentrating without effort, until your mind has learned to block, quite automatically, all intruding stimuli. Only when you can maintain this state of focused attention effortlessly should you go on to Phase II.

The United Mind

The state called yoga (meaning "union") has a generally agreed definition: a "higher" consciousness achieved through a fully awake and relaxed mind.

**Robert Keith Wallace
and Herbert Benson**

The End is Harmony

Many things
that start off easily
end in misery.
Meditation
starts with difficulty
and ends in pleasure
bliss harmony.

Bernard Gunther

The Rightness of Things

Spiritual awakening is the difficult process whereby the increasing realization that everything is as wrong as it can be flips suddenly into the realization that everything is as right as it can be. Or better, everything is as It as it can be.

Alan Watts

A Deeper Wisdom

There is an element of wisdom to be learned from the mystical way of feeling, which does not seem to be attainable in any other manner. If this be the truth, mysticism is to be commended as an attitude toward life, not as a creed about the world ... Even the cautious and patient investigation of truth by science, which seems the very antithesis of the mystic's swift certainty, may be fostered and nourished by that very spirit of reverence in which mysticism lives and moves.

Bertrand Russell

43.
Meditation II

GOAL

To complete the process initiated by the preceding exercise for the purpose of reaching mind levels of transcendental awareness.

TIME

Allow 30 minutes to one hour.

PREPARATION

Sitting or lying comfortably, go into your deepest trance level by two—or more—successive counts from ten to zero, suggesting to yourself that at each count of zero you will have reached a still deeper level. Be conscious of your body's total, comfortable immobility, and suggest to yourself that you will remain immobile throughout the following exercise, unless some emergency should make motion necessary.

This immobility will be very comfortable; you will have no wish to move at all; in fact, you will become nearly oblivious of your body for the duration of the exercise.

THE EXERCISE

As soon as you have reached your deepest trance level, allow the familiar vase to emerge behind your closed lids. Study it briefly once more, then slowly, very gradually, allow it to fade from sight, becoming dimmer and dimmer and dimmer, until at last all trace of it has disappeared.

Now your mind is quite empty of images, of words, and of concepts. Remain in this void, completely relaxed and at ease, completely passive, quietly expectant.

Truly Alone

In every soul . . . there is an "abyss of mystery." Each person has his abyss of which he is not aware, which he cannot know. When hidden things shall have been revealed to us, according to the Promise, there will be unimaginable surprises . . . The least of our actions resounds down to infinite depths, and causes to shudder all the living and all the dead, in such a way that each one among the billions of human beings is truly alone before God. Such is the abyss of our souls, such is their mystery.

Léon Bloy

Reorienting the Mind

Most Westerners are born and bred in Christianity, and have in early years been habituated to the practice of prayer. The word has many meanings, varying with the spiritual development of the individual, but save in the true mystic its essence is always supplication to some external Being or Power. In meditation, however, there is no such element of importuning, of begging for what one has not. At the best the method of prayer is a yearning of the heart; meditation, on the other hand, reorientates the mind, thereby producing the knowledge by which all that is rightly wanted is acquired.

Christmas Humphreys

A Way of Seeing

Contemplation is not the act of looking at the world and seeing something different. Contemplation is simply a different way of seeing. Contemplation is the act of doubting what seems obvious to everyone. Contemplation refuses to live on the surface of things. It is going down and lifting up. It is the act of seeing death where there seems only to be life; seeing life where there seems only to be death.

James Carroll

Breaking-Through

In my breaking-through, . . . I transcend all creatures and am neither God nor creature: I am what I was and I shall remain now and forever. Then I receive an impulse which carries me above all angels. In this impulse I conceive such passing riches that I am not content with God as being God, as being all his godly works, for in this breaking-through I find that God and I are both the same . . .

Meister Eckhart

Presently this void, this emptiness which is your mind, will begin to fill with images you have not seen before, thoughts you have not thought before. Do not reflect on them, do not attempt to integrate them into the thinking processes of your ordinary self. Accept them receptively, unquestioningly, and follow where they lead. The more passively you accept their guidance, the more surely they will lead you deeper into this new, higher realm, where all things have undreamt-of dimensions of vividness, of lucidity, and of unity.

Give your mind leeway to draw on the collective unconscious knowledge of all mankind; you will thereby become aware, with every fiber of your being, of the unity and interrelatedness which joins all fragments of the universe.

Allow this awareness to grow without interference from your intellectualizing self. Your perceptions will grow more and more vivid, your sense of the reality of this higher realm more and more immediate. Let yourself float in this blissful state.

When you feel yourself tiring from the intensity of the experience, slowly bring yourself back to your reality state by two (or more) counts of one to three. Tell yourself that at the end of the first count you will have reached the half-way mark; at the end of the second count you will open your eyes and will be back in your customary reality state. You will be completely alert and completely relaxed at the same time, with the afterglow of your experience still forming a background of happiness within you. You will feel in perfect health, as you will always feel on returning to the everyday reality plane after exploring this new-found dimension of self.

Issa, selection from *Of This World: A Poet's Life in Poetry*, ed. by Richard Lewis, The Dial Press, copyright ©1968 by Richard Lewis.

Heinrich Jacoby, quoted in "Awakening the Body" by Charlotte Selver, from *Explorations in Human Potentialities*, ed. by Herbert A. Otto, copyright ©1966 by Charles C. Thomas.

William James, selections from *The Varieties of Religious Experience*, Longmans, Green, and Co., 1925, copyright ©1902 by William James.

Job 42:1-5, taken from *The Living Bible*, Tyndale House Publishers, copyright ©1971 by Tyndale House Publishers.

Sidney M. Jourard, selections from "Growing Awareness and Awareness of Growth" in *Ways of Growth: Approaches to Expanding Awareness*, ed. by Herbert Otto and John Mann, Grossman Publishers, copyright ©1968 by Herbert Otto and John Mann. Reprinted by permission of Grossman Publishers.

C. G. Jung, selections from "On Psychological Understanding" in the *Journal of Abnormal Psychology*, 1915; and from *Psychology and Religion*, copyright ©1938 by Yale University Press; and from *Memories, Dreams, Reflections*, copyright ©1961, 1962, 1963 by Random House, Inc.

Diane Jurkovic, selection from *1970 Poetry Search Anthology*, collected by Kathleen C. Mellor and Charles E. Schaefer, copyright ©1970 Creativity Center, Fordham University. Reprinted by permission.

Robert Kastenbaum, selections from "Age: Getting There Ahead of Time" in *Psychology Today*, December, 1971, copyright ©1971 by Communications Research Machines, Inc.

Søren Kierkegaard, selection from *A Kierkegaard Anthology*, ed. by Robert Bretall, Princeton, 1946.

R. D. Laing, selection from *The Politics of Experience*, Pantheon Books, Inc., copyright ©1967 by R. D. Laing.

Leslie LeCron, selection from "Hypnosis in the Production of Psi Phenomena" in the *International Journal of Parapsychology*, Vol. III, No. 3, Summer, 1961.

Jennette Lee, selections from *This Magic Body*, The Viking Press, copyright ©1946 by Jennette Lee.

George B. Leonard, selection from *Education and Ecstasy*, Delacorte Press, copyright ©1968 by George B. Leonard.

John C. Lilly, selections from "From Dolphins to LSD—A Conversation with John Lilly" by Sam Keen in *Psychology Today*, December, 1971, copyright ©1972 by Communications Research Machines, Inc.

García Lorca, selection from *The Poetic Image in Don Luis de Góngora*.

Amy Lowell, selections from "The Process of Making Poetry" in *Poetry and Poets*.

Gay Luce and Erik Peper, selections from "Mind Over Body, Mind Over Mind," in *New York Times*, September 12, 1971, Magazine Section.

Peter Marin, selection from *The Free People*, copyright ©1969 by Outerbridge & Dienstfrey.

Abraham H. Maslow, selection from *Religions, Values and Peak Experiences*, copyright ©1964 by Ohio State University Press.

Edward Maupin, quoted in "What Meditation Can Do For You" by Eleanor Criswell in *New Woman* Magazine, copyright ©1971 by Allied Publications, Inc.

Rolly May, selections from *Man's Search For Himself*, copyright ©1953 by W. W. Norton & Co., Inc.

Thomas Merton, selections from *Zen and the Birds of Appetite*, New Directions Pub. Corp., copyright ©1968 by The Abbey of Gethsemane, Inc.; and from *No Man Is an Island*, Harcourt Brace Jovanovich, Inc., copyright ©1955 by The Abbey of Our Lady of Gethsemane.

Desmond Morris, selection from *Intimate Behavior*, Random House, Inc., copyright ©1972 by Desmond Morris.

Gardner Murphy, selection from "Psychology in the Year 2000" in *American Psychologist*, 1969.

F. W. H. Myers, selection from *Fragments of Inner Life: An Autobiographical Sketch*, London, The Society for Psychical Research, 1961.

Friedrich Nietzsche, from *A Treasury of the World's Great Letters*, ed. by M. Lincoln Schuster, copyright ©1940 by Simon & Schuster, Inc.

P. Noy, selection from "The Psychodynamic Meaning of Music — Part IV," *Journal of Music Therapy*, September 1967, IV, copyright ©1967 by The National Association for Music Therapy.

Ladislas M. Orsy, selections from *The Lord of Confusion*, Dimension Books, Inc., copyright ©1970 by Ladislas M. Orsy.

Herbert A. Otto, selections from "Sensory Awakening Through Smell, Touch, and Taste," in *Ways of Growth: Approaches to Expanding Awareness*, ed. by Herbert Otto and John Mann, Grossman Publishers, copyright ©1968 Herbert Otto and John Mann. Reprinted by permission of Grossman Publishers.

Sidney Parnes, selection from *Kaiser Aluminum News*, Vol. 25, No. 3, copyright ©1967 by Kaiser Aluminum & Chemical Corporation.

E. Allison Peers, from *Spirit of Flame: A Study of St. John of the Cross*, Student Christian Movement Press, Ltd.

Charles Anders Peirce, selection from *Philosophical Writings of Peirce*, comp. and ed. by Justus Buchler, copyright ©1955 by Dover Publications, Inc.

Michael Polanyi, selection from *The Study of Man*, The University of Chicago Press, copyright ©1959 by the University College of North Staffordshire.

Thomas E. Powers, selections from "The Ultimate Experiment—How to Find God" in *24 Magazine*, May, 1971.

Richard M. Prodey, poem used with permission of the author.

Ira Progoff, selections from "The Role of Parapsychology in Modern Thinking" in *International Journal of Parapsychology*, Vol. I, No. 1, Summer, 1959.

Magda Proskauer, selections from "Breathing Therapy" in *Ways of Growth: Approaches to Expanding Awareness*, ed. by Herbert Otto and John Mann, Grossman Publishers, copyright©1968 by Herbert Otto and John Mann. Reprinted by permission of Grossman Publishers.

H. L. Puxley, selections from "The Church and the Paranormal" in the *International Journal of Parapsychology*, Vol. VIII, No. 2, Spring 1966.

Karl Rahner, selection from *Encounters With Silence*, copyright©1960 by Paulist-Newman Press.

Theodore Roszak, selection from *Sources*, Harper & Row, Publishers, copyright©1972 by Theodore Roszak.

Dane Rudhyar, selection from *The Pulse of Life*, Shambala Publications, copyright©1970 by Dane Rudhyar.

Bertrand Russell, selection from *Mysticism and Logic*, Barnes & Noble, Inc., 1954.

Milan Ryzl, selection from *Parapsychology*, Hawthorn Books, Inc., copyright©1970 by Milan Ryzl.

George Santayana, selection from *The Idler and His Works*, Goerge Braziller, Inc.

Stephen M. Schoen, selection from "LSD and Creative Attention" in *Ways of Growth: Approaches to Expanding Awareness*, ed. by Herbert Otto and John Mann. Reprinted by permission of Grossman Publishers.

Charlotte Selver, selections from *Explorations in Human Potentialities*, ed. by Herbert A. Otto, Charles C. Thomas, copyright©1966 by Herbert A. Otto.

Mrs. Upton Sinclair, selections quoted in *Parapsychology* by Milan Ryzl, Hawthorn Books, Inc., copyright©1970 by Milan Ryzl.

Maurice Solovine, quoted in *Einstein—The Life and Times*, World Publishing Company, copyright©1971 by Ronald W. Clark.

Kilton Stewart, selections from *Creative Psychology and Dream Education*, Stewart Foundation for Creative Psychology, copyright© Mrs. Clara Stewart Flagg. Used by permission of Kilton Stewart's widow, Mrs. Clara Stewart Flagg.

Student Committee on Mental Health, Princeton University, selection from *Psychedelics and the College Student*, copyright©1967 by Princeton University Press.

Pierre Teilhard de Chardin, selections from *The Phenomenon of Man*, copyright©1959 by Wm. Collins Sons & Co., Ltd. and Harper & Row, Publishers Inc.; from *Hymn of the Universe*, copyright©1965 by Wm. Collins Sons & Co., Ltd., London, and Harper & Row, Publishers; and from *The Divine Milieu*, copyright©1960 by Wm. Collins Sons & Co., and Harper & Row, Publishers.

Nyanaponika Thera, selection from *The Heart*, quoted in *Zen and the Birds of Appetite* by Thomas Merton, New Directions Pub. Corp., copyright©1968 by The Abbey of Gethsemane, Inc.

William Irwin Thompson, selection from *At the Edge of History*, Harper & Row, Publishers, copyright©1971 by William Irwin Thompson.

Upanishads, selections from *The Upanishads*, Penguin Books, Inc., copyright©1965 by Juan Mascaró.

Bill Voyd, selection from *Shelter and Society*, ed. by Paul Oliver, copyright©1969 by Praeger Publishers, Inc.

August H. Wagner, selection from "Reincarnation" in the *International Journal of Parapsychology*, Vol. X, No. 3, Autumn, 1968.

Robert Keith Wallace and Herbert Benson, selection from "The Physiology of Meditation" in *Scientific American*, February, 1972, copyright©1972 by Scientific American, Inc.

Alan Watts, selections from *This Is It*, The Macmillan Co., copyright©1958, 1960 by Alan W. Watts; from *The Joyous Cosmology*, copyright©1962 by Pantheon Books; and from *Nature, Man and Woman*, copyright©1958 by Pantheon Books, Inc.

Minor White, selection from "Extended Perception Through Photography and Suggestion" in *Ways of Growth: Approaches to Expanding Awareness*, ed. by Herbert Otto and John Mann, Grossman Publishers, copyright©1968 by Herbert Otto and John Mann. Reprinted by permission of Grossman Publishers.

Lancelot Law Whyte, selection from "Science and Our Understanding of Ourselves" in *Science and Public Affairs, the Bulletin of the Atomic Scientists*, copyright©1971 by the Educational Foundation for Nuclear Science.

Yüan-chou, selection from *Essays in Zen Buddhism* by D. T. Suzuki, Vol. 2, Grove Press, 1961.

Photo Credits

Leslie Becker 139; Peter Clemens 68, 75, 137, 206; Paul Conklin 97; Maury Englander 36-37, 189; Mimi Forsyth 14, 18, 31, 52, 67, 80, 93, 98, 105, 106, 113, 115, 119, 129, 131, 132, 141, 144, 157, 169, 170, 180, 193, 196, 209, 215; Cynthia Grey 29; Peter Karas 17, 22, 27, 79, 123, 165, 179, 187; Algimantas Kezys 34, 63, 72, 83, 89, 94, 102, 125, 135, 149, 153, 161, 166, 173, 195, 200, 211, 212, 219; Joyce Macksoud 59; Michael Mangan 12, 84, 101, 116, 143, 147, 216; Sylvia Plachy 90, 174; George Roos 57, 71, 76, 120, 183, 204, 221; Dave Sagarin 21; Bob Smith 51, 198.

77 10 9 8 7 6